GREAT-HEARTED

Grieving Well

Janet Lindsey

WESTBOW
PRESS®
A DIVISION OF THOMAS NELSON
& ZONDERVAN

WestBow Press books may be ordered through booksellers or by contacting:

WestBow Press
A Division of Thomas Nelson & Zondervan
1663 Liberty Drive
Bloomington, IN 47403
www.westbowpress.com
1 (866) 928-1240

ISBN: 978-1-9736-4349-4 (sc)
ISBN: 978-1-9736-4350-0 (hc)
ISBN: 978-1-9736-4251-0 (e)

Library of Congress Control Number: 2018912654

Print information available on the last page.

WestBow Press rev. date: 10/30/2018

Contents

Acknowledgments

The story of how this Bible study came to be written and the way God orchestrated events and placed people in my path according to His timing and will is amazing. But isn't God amazing? I am in awe of His providence and His working in and through our lives. To Him be all the glory!

I want to dedicate this Bible study to Diane Egbers and Lee Ann Easter, whose friendship and encouragement gave me the inspiration to share my journey with the purpose of helping others who are suffering in their loss. I graciously acknowledge the time each has spent motivating, supporting, and praying for me in this process. I am so thankful God placed them in my life. They are a joy to know, and I love them both.

Introduction

In April 2009, our twenty-two-year-old son, Gary, and only child went fishing after work one Wednesday afternoon. He was an avid fisherman, having won many local tournaments. Gary was an excellent fisherman because he studied about fish, water temperatures, moon phases, spawning habits, and other techniques that increased his knowledge and improved his ability on the water. His life dream was to become a professional fisherman.

This April day was cool and extremely windy. According to other fishermen who were out in their boats, the waters were rough. From what we can tell, Gary stopped for some reason and left his boat idling. Somehow, and we do not know how, he fell out of his boat. The water temperature was in the fifties. He had layers of clothing on. Even though my son took years of swimming lessons and was an excellent swimmer, the elements, heavy clothing, and the fact that he wasn't wearing a life jacket were too much for him.

A passerby on the bridge above noticed an unmanned boat idling in circles on the water below. He turned around and went back to the spot to confirm what he was seeing, then called 911.

This is where our nightmare began.

For three days and three nights, they searched for our son. On the third day, in late afternoon, they found him in thirty feet of water close to where the boat was first seen. Because it was an accident, an autopsy had to be performed. They discovered nothing but water in the lungs. After a week, we were able to have a funeral, and the next day a burial.

Our life suddenly and tragically changed that day. Extreme grief was new to us. It was proving unbearable. We wanted to hide from it, escape it somehow, anything but endure this anguish of heart and soul! *What do we do now? How do we live? Will we survive another day, another hour, the next moment?*

Since I was in my late twenties, I have been involved with in-depth Bible studies. As soon as I finished one study, I would have another scheduled. The week before my son's accident, I had just completed facilitating a study on God's providence and thought I was all the wiser now, having more understanding on this subject. While I was at the lake those three days, many times over I thought about God's providence and how I was completely clueless. I felt that everything I had ever learned about God had just been thrown out with my loss. *Who are You, God? Why have You allowed this? I'm confused. I'm hurt. I'm angry.* All the dreams my son had for his life instantly vanished!

This is the first Bible study I've written. I wish there was no need for a Bible study on grief. Sadly, devastating loss has dramatically changed our lives. In the early days of my grief, I searched the Christian bookstores for a Bible study on this subject. My emotional state couldn't bear the fellowship of a group setting, and I chose to study alone. I was dying inside from my loss and knew I needed to search the scriptures in order to survive. I never found what I was looking for in the bookstore that day, so I continued to pour my heart into God's Word and in dialogue with Him. I voiced my complaints, my heartache, my disappointments, my anger, and my confusion. God kept directing me to verses of scripture that comforted me and gave me hope; verses that brought me to Him. I started a journal to record my thoughts and scriptures that encouraged me. I read others' stories on grief and related to them.

I distinctly remember one afternoon sitting on my front porch reading an account of a woman who had lost her teenage son in an auto accident. Most of what she said was so much of how I was feeling and what I was going through. My weeping became so hard I felt I couldn't breathe. Reading her story was hard but also comforting and made me aware I was not alone in my grief. There were others suffering as well, and God has promised to never leave or forsake me.

This study is from my experience on the subject of grief. Although I have not conquered grief, I have progressed and learned to live in this new way of life. I have seen God working to move me forward. If I can help one person in his or her journey to draw closer to Jesus and find hope and strength in Him, then my grief has purpose. My desire is to point a hurting heart to Jesus. He is our source of life, abundant life where you can thrive and not just survive.

For the benefit of the reader, included at the close of each session is a personal story of loss from a grieving parent, spouse, child, or sibling. These willing participants have found strength in helping others in their great time of need. They have come from tragedy and loss and have been transformed by the healing power of Jesus. I am thankful for their input and pray their stories uplift and encourage you.

This study points a grieving heart to Jesus. There is no way I have covered all aspects of grief. It is an endless subject. Furthermore, too long a study would be overwhelming for those suffering. Whether you choose to study in a group setting (leader guide included) or alone in the privacy of your home, this study is suitable. You will need your Bibles to look up scripture passages. Meditate on the verses in each session. Absorb them in your soul. Use a commentary if you like, as it will broaden the meaning of many verses. You will find God. He says, "You will seek me and find me when you seek me with all your heart. I will be found by you" (Jeremiah

29:13, 14a). He also says, "My word that goes out from my mouth: It will not return to me empty, but will accomplish what I desire and achieve the purpose for which I sent it" (Isaiah 55:11). God has something to say to you. Open your aching heart to Him.

Start your study each day in prayer. Desperate people cry out to God. Don't be ashamed to cry out for Him. Ask Him to show you His ways and what He wants to say to you through His Word and His Spirit.

The title of this study expresses what is needed in order to know how to live within our loss, all while finding joy and strength to carry on. *Great-hearted* means courageous, generous, bold, fearless, brave, and valiant! God will give us the courage and bravery to move forward and glorify Him in and through our losses.

Oh friend in grief, journey with me to a closer walk with God. May He bless you and keep you tenderly in His comfort and care.

Session 1

You Are Not Alone

God, You have ripped my heart to pieces! I feel alone.[1]

He gathers the lambs in his arms and carries them close to his heart.
—Isaiah 40:11

God makes a home for the lonely.
—Psalm 68:6 (NASB)

Turn to me and be gracious to me, for I am
lonely and afflicted. The troubles
of my heart have multiplied; free me from my anguish.
—Psalm 25:16–17

One of the most distinguishable aspects of grief and loss is loneliness. Your grief is your very own. It can't be shared. No one but you can possibly know the depths of your loss, your pain, your heart, and your thoughts. Your loss is a personal journey that sometimes makes you feel lonely and forsaken. Those who have traveled this path can empathize with you, but no one knows how you truly suffer.

I remember the day I felt separated from all I had ever known. If the separation from my son was not enough to bear already, the disconnection from life in general was overwhelming. That is when I felt I was losing myself. I was driving down a crowded highway and crying, "I can't deal with this! God, please help me!" I considered pulling over but couldn't break free from the traffic. I honestly thought I was mentally and emotionally crashing.

This grief journey at times is solitary. There are circumstances we have to wrestle with alone, in the deep recesses of our hearts and minds. Although others may help us to a point, only God can minister to our every need in ways that are beyond our understanding. We are earthen vessels to be used by God for His purposes. He may link your life with counselors or others who are walking along similar paths to help you in this journey. However, God is your greatest strength. He will never abandon or forsake you. He provides the care and comforts you long for so deeply.

How have you felt there is no escaping from this grief and loneliness?

_____

_____

_____

When the sting of adversity overwhelms us, the sense of isolation moves into our souls. We believe that we have been abandoned and that no one understands our agony. We seem lost without our loved one's presence. It is vital at this point to recall the promises of God that minister to this great need.

In Isaiah 40:11 is the picture of our Great Shepherd carrying His lambs, the ones who are sorrowful and have collapsed under the weight of grief so that they can't get up. He tenderly cares for these.

From Genesis to Revelation, the Bible uses the illustration of God as our Shepherd and Jesus as our Good Shepherd, and we are the sheep. Sheep must have a shepherd, or they will die. They will walk off a cliff without guidance. They are defenseless from predators and are vulnerable, helpless, and easily influenced creatures. A great shepherd will give every resource he has to take care of his sheep.

Let's look at some verses about how our Shepherd cares for His sheep.

- Psalm 23 is often quoted at funerals to comfort the grieving. As our Shepherd, He can tenderly care for us in rest, in peace, through guidance, in the fear of death and the fear that death brings, in mercy, and in loneliness. God is always with us.
- Matthew 9:35–36 reveals our Savior's compassionate heart for His sheep. This passage also tells us that we are a needy flock who require help even with our basic needs.
- Revelation 7:17 brings us hope that we will be released from the agony of grief, and God Himself will wipe away our tears.
- John 10:1–16 is a beautiful illustration of the Shepherd and His flock and how He takes us unto Himself as our great provider. However, these verses make very clear the reality that in order to have our needs met, we must be in a relationship with the Shepherd. Then we can hear His voice. Then He goes ahead of us to lead and guide in the right path, and we follow as we hear His voice. The Shepherd lays down His life for the sheep, whom He knows intimately and personally.

Which verses from the four passages above speak most to you today? Where are you in your grief, and how do you find the passages to be a comfort and encouragement that God will use every resource you need to care for you?

_____

_____

_____

I have found that these passages affect me differently according to my level of grief. What you may write today may be different from what you write later. Reflect again after a week and see which verse is speaking to your heart on that day.

> A father of the fatherless and a judge for the widows, Is God in His holy habitation. God makes a home for the lonely. (Psalm 68:5–6 NASB)

Not only is God our great Shepherd, but He is also our compassionate, all-sufficient God. Perhaps you have lost a parent or a spouse. These verses tell us that God is our heavenly Father who can come in our distress. He is "a father of the fatherless." He is our guardian.

Another place in scripture where God is our defender is Proverbs 23:10–11 (NLT): "Don't take the land of defenseless orphans. For their Redeemer is strong; he himself will bring their charges against you."

He has also been referred to as our husband (Isaiah 54:5), the one who can meet our every need, and our spiritual provider. Jesus is referred to in the New Testament as the Bridegroom, and His people are the bride. Our God is jealous for His very own with a godly jealousy. Through His power and His tender compassion, He comforts us in our lonely condition. He is our protector.

In Luke 7:11–17 (MSG), Jesus was entering a town called Nain. His disciples and a crowd of people were with Him.

As they approached the village gate, they met a funeral procession—a woman's only son was being carried out for burial. And the mother was a widow. When Jesus saw her, his heart broke. He said to her, "Don't cry."

This woman's tears caused Jesus's heart to hurt. What a tragic and sad situation for her! How alone she must have felt! Yet Jesus knew He was going to raise her son back to life and relieve her suffering.

Our tears make His heart hurt too. He sees our situations and wants us to know that our loved ones who have died in Him are raised to life again because Jesus has conquered death. We will see them again one day.

I have experienced loneliness from losing my son. I miss him terribly. I wrote about one of these times in my book *Therefore, Hope.*

Sometimes when Ed (my husband) and I are together, I have a loneliness that enters my heart. It is for our son and our true home. I went a long time without mentioning this to him. One evening, while we were sitting in the swing in our quiet, peaceful backyard, this emotion came over me again. I wanted to tell him about it, so I said, "Sometimes I have this feeling, especially when we are together …" But before I could finish the sentence, he answered and said, "A lonely feeling." I said, "Yes! It's like for Gary and heaven." He said, "I have it too." It's a loneliness we can't fill for each other. We yearn for our son and our real home, "for love is as strong as Death" (Song of Songs 8:6).[2]

Describe the loneliness you may be experiencing.

_____

_____

_____

At the end of this session, Becky's story tells of losing grandparents, two husbands, a brother, and her parents. Her story will encourage a lonely heart.

The psalms are windows into our souls. They often mirror our struggles, which is why we relate so easily to them. Life is hard, and we need such words from the psalmist to speak directly to our hurting hearts. Psalm 25:16–17 finds David pouring out his heart to God.

> Turn to me and be gracious to me, for I am lonely and afflicted. The troubles of my heart have multiplied; free me from my anguish.

I have recited this prayer to God with tears streaming down my face and an exclamation mark at the end. I needed relief right then. I desired deliverance, but knowing my circumstances were not going to change, I needed to learn to live within them.

Although my family and friends were comforting and helpful and would have done anything for me, I had to learn to rely on God and the strength and peace only He could bring me. The key to relying on God is in verse 15 of this same passage: "My eyes are ever on the LORD." Loneliness can come from knowing no one understands your grief and the depth of your hurt. But God does! That is why we should rely on Him.

We are not meant to go through this life alone. We need each other, our families, our friends, and our local churches. Our church family was and still is such a source of strength and comfort to us. They stood by us and prayed for us. Even though some may not have understood our depth of grief and loss, they were our support and walked many hard days alongside us. Referring to the story of the widow whose only son had died (Luke 7:11–17), the people of the town surrounded her with comfort and support.

Dear friends in grief, keeping our eyes fixed on Jesus will give us more endurance than we can imagine. It is so important in our relationship with the Lord to know we can bring all our sorrow and hurt to Him. He knows our hearts are broken and can help us in our great time of loss. Take heart, dear one in grief, for you are not alone on this journey.

God's Faithful Personal Promise

Write out Joshua 1:9

_____

_____

_____

Write out Deuteronomy 31:8

_____

_____

_____

This promise made to Moses and Joshua and quoted again in the New Testament in Hebrews 13 still applies to all believers today. So, believe it, take comfort in it, and rest, knowing that God is continually with you. You are not alone!

Journal Quote:

> To read the works of others who have gone through grief is another way of keeping the process going, and of finding another understanding friend. When a writer describes for

me how I am feeling, she or he becomes my friend; I am
not alone. Somehow that person has achieved some peace
with the pain, enough to write it down. Maybe I, too, will
find my way through this.[3] (Martha Whitmore Hickman)

Becky's Story

Many books have been written on the subject of grief. It is a subject I wish I knew nothing about and did not have firsthand experience with. I lost older grandparents when I was young but no one whose life was closely connected to mine. So unexpected and devastating to me was the sudden death of my husband—my high school sweetheart and daddy to our two-and-a-half-year-old son. We were both twenty-eight years old at that time. In the blink of an eye, my whole world had changed. Not only was I a widow, but I also became both a mother and father to my young son. I often told folks I was not a single parent; I had the Lord guiding me all the way. It was not an easy time in my life, far from it, but with God's grace and strength, I was able to get through it. This year marks the thirty-second anniversary of his death. It seems like a lifetime ago.

Over the next several years, I lost a brother, and then my mother and then my father. My parents died in the same year. I was the youngest in a big family, so my parents were somewhat older. They had been relatively healthy but developed some health issues at the end of their lives. Both their deaths were unexpected. I was very saddened by the deaths of my family members, but I had already experienced such an overwhelming loss that I don't think it hit me as hard as it did my other family members. Again, God carried me through these difficult times and gave me comfort.

Seven years after the death of my first husband, I remarried. God blessed me with a wonderful Christian man. What an amazing gift from God! With this marriage, I gained two sons and a daughter. My son was now ten years old. I went from a family of two to a family of six, not an easy task. But again, God blessed me with the putting together of a blended family. For several years, we enjoyed life, we worked, and we raised our children. Eventually, the children were grown and on their own. We did not mind that we were empty nesters. We had earned it!

Church was an important part of our lives. We rarely missed a service. My husband taught a Sunday school class for twenty-five years. It was primarily made of our age group, but we had all ages. He was a gifted teacher with great Bible knowledge, and he also had a way of building relationships. Not only did he teach the Word of God, but he had the ability to make long-lasting friendships. He wanted to make folks feel loved and let them know that they were important to him and to the Lord.

Everyone wants their happily ever after and to grow old with the one they love. That doesn't always happen. For me, the husband God had so graciously given me was going to be called to his heavenly home much sooner than either one of us had anticipated. How could that be?

It was a normal Sunday morning; we were getting ready for church and making plans for the afternoon. David began to have breathing problems, an ambulance was called, and last words were spoken. A man who exercised on the treadmill almost daily and could lift 215 pounds in the weight room was suddenly gone. Pulmonary embolism was listed as the cause of death for my sixty-two-year-old husband.

Now, the reason I am sharing my grief experiences with you is not to gain your sympathy or sadness for me. I want to offer hope for you and your life ahead. If you are reading this, you are most likely seeking help and knowledge on how you are going to get through your own grief process.

The death of a loved one is overwhelming. When it is a sudden death, it is such a shock that you think you will surely die. However, God is there to give us His peace and comfort. If you have accepted Jesus as your Lord and Savior, He is there to give you strength. There is verse after verse of scripture in the Bible. These are promises made by God that you can claim and believe. Psalm 147:3 says, "He heals the brokenhearted and binds up their wounds."

Going through a grieving process is not easy but has to be done. There are no shortcuts, no quick fixes. Grief has many symptoms. Besides just being brokenhearted, it affects so many aspects of your body. You are physically tired and emotionally drained. Your heart feels so heavy that it really hurts. It's hard to breathe, hard to concentrate on anything, and hard to accomplish the simplest tasks. You have to be kind to yourself and allow your body to make adjustments to your new life. Sadly, it is a *new* life. Your old life is no longer available to you, but God is still in control and has a plan for your life. He loves you and will see you through your time of sorrow.

Is it easy? No, it is not. Will the sorrow become easier to bear? Yes, it will. Do I still struggle some days? Yes, I do. Am I healing? Yes, I am.

I would be foolish to think I will forget all that I have been through. At the same time, I will always remember that it is only by God's grace that I have made it this far. It has been two years and four months. There are days when it seems so much fresher in my mind. On those days, my strength truly comes from the Lord. Because God saved me many years ago, I have the blessed assurance that I will one day see Jesus face-to-face. I find great comfort in knowing I will meet my loved ones in heaven and spend eternity there.

God is faithful. He continues to send blessings into my life. I'm filled with joy to say that my son and daughter-in-law are expecting their first child, a son, in September.

One last thing that I will tell you. If you have not been saved and do not have a personal relationship with Jesus, your journey is going to be very tough, almost impossible. I urge you to contact someone who can give you the help you need to invite Jesus into your heart. You won't regret it.[4]

Psalm 18:28 says, "You, LORD, keep my lamp burning; my God turns my darkness into light."

Journal

Session 2

God Is Good, So Why Has This Happened?

Where were You that night when I begged for my son to be alive? Where were You for three days while they searched for him? Why would You allow us to live three days not knowing if our son would ever be found? Why did we have to endure the thought of him under cold, dark waters? This part of You, God, I don't know. I have never experienced You like this.[1]

Then Job replied to the LORD: "I know that you can do all things; no plan of yours can be thwarted." You asked, "Who is this that obscures my counsel without knowledge?" Surely I spoke of things I did not understand, things too wonderful for me to know.

—Job 42:1–3

When I wrote *Peering through a Mist*, it was within the first two years after my son passed away. My grief was fresh and raw. I struggled with my faith, my responsibilities at work and home, and my relationships. I was confused about my relationship with God. Who was He, really, that He would allow this tragedy in my life? I questioned Him on many things concerning my son's tragic accident, and I asked the universal question of *why* many times over. But God is not the author of confusion. There was something I needed to learn about Him. In my struggles, I asked, "Who are You, God?" I thought I knew Him, but now I was experiencing Him in a whole different way.

While it is important to have a Bible study on grief and how to cope with the daily struggles of every aspect that comes with it, it is of utmost importance to know God. Without God, nothing makes sense, especially our grief. I'm not saying that after you've finished this study, you will understand why you are enduring such a devastating loss and all your questions will be answered, because that is not so. You will, however, come away with a better understanding of who God is through Jesus and how He is the only hope we have.

When we come into a relationship with the living God, we experience a supernatural understanding from His perspective on grief and loss, sin and suffering. This occurs as we spend time in His presence seeking Him and reading His Word. He is the one directing your heart through His Spirit that lives within you. It is exhilarating to know the King of the universe can and does speak to us, through His Word, His Spirit, our circumstances, and godly people. What a precious gift He has given us in His Son and His Holy Spirit.

When Jesus was in the upper room with His disciples, He spoke to them about things that were to come. He said, "The Counselor, the Holy Spirit, whom the Father will send in my name, will teach you all things and will remind you of everything I have said to you" (John 14:26). In my loss and grief, the Holy Spirit did this very thing for me. He reminded me of something He had spoken to my heart twenty-two years earlier. And then I began to experience the next verse, "Peace I leave with you; my peace I give you. I do not give to you as the world gives. Do not let your hearts be troubled and do not be afraid" (verse 27).

If we can grasp that God is sovereign over our circumstances and knows us intimately, more than we know ourselves, this will help in the course of our grief. Even though everything may seem out of control, God is not. Although everything may seem surreal and different from before your loss, God is the same; He never changes.

Job is a grand example of this. I am so thankful we have his story of heartache, grief, and loss of everything. He suffered immensely but not without reason. God allowed it. He even introduced Job to Satan (Job 1:6–8). Although Job was righteous and was pleasing to the Lord, he suffered beyond my ability to comprehend. God in His permissive will allowed, even initiated, Job's trials.

The verse that comes to mind is Isaiah 55:8–9. Write out this verse.

_____

_____

Are you experiencing a lack of understanding of God's ways right now in your struggles?

Does anything make sense to you? Sometimes it helps to write out how we are feeling. Although it may be difficult to express your thoughts, try as best you can to explain how your circumstances are perplexing.

_____

_____

Although Job was never given an explanation of his trials and sorrow, God revealed Himself through them. And then Job was able to say, "Surely I spoke of things I did not understand, things too wonderful for me to know" (Job 42:3).

Over time spent in God's presence and in His Word, He will show His faithfulness to you, even through your loss. Allow Him this time. He knows more than us what is best and will show His strength through our weaknesses.

Shortly after my son's passing, one of our ministers at church kept repeating the phrase, "God is good all the time," to which we were to respond, "All the time, God is good." I found I couldn't say that. I was struggling with the "good" part. How could He be good after allowing this tragedy in my life? I wrote about this in my book *Therefore, Hope.*

It is so much easier to write about the trials of life and how to depend on God to get through them than it is to live them out. It is easy to say God is good when you have not been through the fires of hell and wrestled with the question of Is He really Good? It is so much easier to say, Be thankful in everything than it is to be thankful in a tragedy that has taken the life of your child. It is so much easier to say, Rejoice in the Lord when everything is good and going your way than it is to rejoice when your world has fallen apart, and you're trying to reconcile how God's perfect love fits into the horror of the darkest nights of your life.[2]

The Bible has many verses proclaiming God's goodness. Our minister was right in what he said. Sometimes those of us struggling to understand this have to fight to get to a place where we understand His goodness ... from a different perspective. God is good regardless of our circumstances. Someone might ask how anyone could ever question whether God is good or not. Perhaps it arises from the question as to why bad things happen to good people.

Is this a struggle for you? Why or why not?

_____

_____

_____

_____

Ed's story at the end of this session is one of struggling to understand. He walks us through his journey of questions with no answers that brought him into a deeper relationship with Jesus. He stresses that a loving God can handle all our questions and confusion and that we need to pour our hearts out to Him.

When God created the heaven and earth and everything in them, He said it was good. His perfect will was for humankind to live in harmony with Him and all creation. We were created to love God, worship Him, serve Him, and be in relationship with Him. Our work was to be enjoyable and pleasant. This is His perfect will. Everything God created was perfect and good.

Sorrowfully, it didn't stay perfect and good very long, and sin entered the world. Along with it came death, sorrow, pain, sickness, and hate. All of creation has suffered the effects of sin. Sadly, our original parents made the wrong choice. Adam and Eve had every need met by God, and yet they wanted more. When they sinned, it was rebellion against God. They believed the lie of the devil instead of what God had said. Ever since that day, we have suffered the consequences. We live in a world where tragedies take place that God has allowed. Sin is devastating. In my Bible concordance, there are 210 verses on sin! I believe God wants us to understand what sin does and how we can overcome its snare.

Since there is sin, there is darkness in our world. Beyond doubt, God hates sin and the consequence it brings about. He hurts when you hurt, and He understands. Sin cost God. The price was the cross where the sinless Christ died. His blood cleanses us from all sin. The Bible says, "Without the shedding of blood there is no forgiveness" (Hebrews 9:22b).

All around us every day, we see the results of living in a sinful world. The good that God intended is still there, but it has been marred with evil. Therefore, God had a plan set in place from the beginning of time to cover our sin and rebellion so that we could be forgiven of our sins and live forever with Him.

Billy Graham said, "From Genesis to Revelation, from earth's greatest tragedy, to earth's greatest triumph, the dramatic story of humanity's lowest depths and God's highest heights can be couched in twenty-five beautiful words: 'For God so loved the world, that He gave His only begotten Son, that whoever believes in Him should not perish but have everlasting life'" (John 3:16 NKJV).[3]

If we want to know God more and what He is like, look at Jesus. He came to show us the Father. Jesus said, "I and the Father are one" (John 10:30) and "Anyone who has seen me has seen the Father" (John 14:9). Jesus is Immanuel, God with us (Isaiah 7:14, Matthew 1:23).

While Jesus was hanging on the cross, with the sins of the world draining His very life, the Father could not look on His Son because of the sin He bore. So much was Jesus's grief when His Father turned His back that he cried out, "My God, my God, why have you forsaken me?" (Mark 15:34b NASB). Jesus was obedient to His Father's will to die for us so that we could be forgiven of sin and have life eternal. The cost was everything. God's grace and love are great for you! Without His grace, love, and mercy, there would be no forgiveness of sins, no salvation, and no eternal life.

None of us deserves God's grace. Grace is the greatest gift God has given us. His grace is greater than any sorrow. He is able to identify with our deepest sorrow. With what He suffered for us, do we not know that He understands our grief and pain? Does He not understand our whys? Is He not our compassionate Savior? Is He not a good God for granting us grace and mercy because of our sin? Yes! The question is not, "Is God good?" but "Why would God love and care so much for us sinners?"

My personal illustrations help me see God's love and grace more clearly. When my son was one year old, he had hernia surgery. Of course, they had to put him to sleep. When they wheeled him out of surgery in a baby bed, his eyes kept trying to focus on me but couldn't quite stay fixed. He was trying to reach for me but kept falling over. I was crying and following him down the hall. I asked if I could just pick him up, and they directed me to a rocking chair where they placed him in my arms. I held him close and kissed his face over and over while consoling him that it would be all right. When he was eleven, he had an endoscopes procedure. Again, he was under anesthesia, which led to severe nausea and vomiting later. All night I tried to make him comfortable, until the doctor finally called in medicine for his relief. As a young man, there was a time when a young lady emotionally hurt him, and the year of his accident, he was given the layoff slip from his job of three years. With all these situations and more, I wanted to take the hurt, pain, and sickness from him so he wouldn't have to suffer. I hurt so much for him. And yes, I would have taken his place in death so that he could live if God had allowed.

Think how much more God loves us than we could possibly love our family and how much He hurts for us and wants us to come to Him for comfort and peace in our suffering, sickness, loss, and broken hearts. He so wants to cradle and rock us in His arms while consoling us that one day all will be made right. Even God chose an illustration of a mother and her child to demonstrate how much He cares for us. "Can a mother forget the baby at her breast and have no compassion on the child she has borne?

Though she may forget, I will not forget you" (Isaiah 49:15). He is telling us that He knows our deepest needs more than a mother knows her own child, and He is never inattentive.

Even though it was difficult writing out my illustration, it also helps me face my grief and see all the ways God's grace has been covering me over the years.

If you feel you can, write out your personal illustration that exhibits God's love and grace for you.

_____

_____

_____

Don't let your circumstances tell you God does not care and He is unaware. Believe the promises from God.

It was God's will to send His Son to die on a cruel cross with the sins of the world weighed down upon Him, so why would it not be in God's will to bruise me for His purposes? Why not me? The bruising will reveal where my relationship is with Jesus Christ. Does my life through my circumstances create a yearning for God in others? Can I let Him break and mold me in ways that draw me closer to Him even while troubled over the lack of understanding on my part and among all the questions that seem to have no answers? Perhaps we can cease with the whys and questions and instead believe that God has entrusted those of us reading this study with great afflictions to not only grow us and to draw others to Him but for even greater use than we could ever imagine. Think of this: everything we do here on earth has eternal purposes. How can our grief bring about God's good purposes through us? Read these verses and write out one of the ways God uses our heartaches for His purposes.

2 Corinthians 1:3–7

_____

_____

Our God is holy, He is faithful, and He is worthy of our worship, praise, time, and devotion. He is infinite and knows all about you and your circumstance. During your time with God this week, delight in Psalm 139 and Matthew 10:29–31. Be reassured of His great love and concern for you.

On this journey in experiencing a deeper relationship with Him in the midst of our grief, and as we learn more about Him and His ways, we can discover all that He has to offer our hurting hearts. The Christian life is not always easy or struggle-free, and at times it would be easy to give up and lose heart. However, we gain endurance as we dwell in His presence. He loves you, dear one, with an everlasting love. His grace will see you through. God is love, and God is good!

God's Faithful Personal Promise

Write out 2 Corinthians 12:8–10

_____

_____

_____

_____

_____

_____

Clearly, Paul's continual struggles were God's will, and because they are recorded for us, we are privileged to read them and see God's faithfulness through his life. God will be faithful in your life too.

Journal Quote:

> The climax of sin is that it crucified Jesus Christ, and what was true in the history of God on earth will be true in your history and in mine. In our mental outlook we have to reconcile ourselves to the fact of sin as the only explanation as to why Jesus Christ came, and as the explanation of the grief and sorrow in life.[4] (Oswald Chambers)

Ed's Story

Lance Evan Russell, our firstborn, made his entrance into this world on November 20, 1997.

For his third birthday party, he was healthy and happy and active. He opened presents and sorted his presents into piles. He got a miniature dachshund puppy for his birthday. He named her Sally. One week later, Lance had a fever, was lethargic, and didn't seem himself at all. We took him to his doctor. Ear and throat infections, we were told. We were given antibiotics to give Lance to help fight the infections. The infections may or may not have gotten better, but his disposition and lethargy did not improve.

Two weeks after his happy, healthy third birthday, we were rushing Lance to the children's hospital, praying that he wouldn't bleed out in his brain and have a stroke before we could get to the emergency room.

He had leukemia, AML. A couple of mornings later, Lance had four areas of bleeding in his brain. After that, his right side hardly worked. His right eye, hand, arm, foot, and leg did not function correctly. His body almost shut down. He had tubes going in and out of everywhere. He was given chemotherapy and radiation. He worked hard to be able to surprise me one day by walking across the hospital room.

He had a bone marrow transplant.

Nothing worked. The doctors at Vanderbilt Children's Hospital advised us to take Lance home and make him as comfortable and happy as we could and to love him as much as possible. We did. Lance died at our home, in our arms at 4:30 a.m. on September 29, 2001. He was three years old.

We had a website set up to allow us to post information about Lance so that we could tell things one time and not repeat information to people calling us on the phone. While Lance was sick, we were asked many questions: "Can I bring Lance some clothes that might fit because the chemotherapy is changing his body?" "What food does Lance enjoy so we can get some gift cards for him?" "What is the address so we can send Lance get-well cards and activity books?"

And there were other questions: "What sin is in your family's life that God has to do this to get your attention and repentance?" "Why don't you step out in faith and get out of the hospital and away from doctors so God can heal your son?" I even had a kindly woman give me a book that gave spiritual reasons for physical diseases. The reason the book gave for childhood leukemia, you might wonder, is the child feels abandoned by the father.

These questions hurt. They seemed brutal. But rather than throw them away, I pursued answers. I spent many nights with my face on the carpet of a Ronald McDonald houseroom, praying to God to heal my son and to help me understand.

One of the questions asked of me was, "Where was your Jesus when your son died?" I don't think the people who asked this question were really interested in where Jesus was on that morning but were trying to make a point that maybe Jesus is not who He says He is. But taking it literally and adding to it, I wanted to find out: where was Jesus when my son died?

Where was Jesus when my son died? Was it truly God's will that my son be diagnosed with cancer and die before his fourth birthday? Was God in control and moving all of us around on a chessboard to accomplish His purpose? Why, when thousands of people were praying for the healing of my son, was God's answer to our prayer still "No"? Is it true that God won't allow me more than I can handle? When Lance was sick and even now fifteen years after he passed away, I had and have questions for God. I wanted some of what we had been through to make sense. I wanted to be able to understand a little better what was going on and why my helpless little boy had to suffer so mightily while living—and ultimately to not live four years. But I had a problem. I didn't want to make God angry at my lack of faith, because I didn't understand, and I wanted so desperately to understand. So, I was stuck with this thought: *Is asking God these types of questions enough to anger Him?*

There are a few ways that God can give us information. God can tell us something in a dream or vision. I have not, to my knowledge, had a vision or dream given to me that answers a question or gives me information. God can speak directly to us. As far as I know, I have never heard God speak to me in an audible way. God can speak to our hearts in a still small voice to guide us. I think I have been nudged by this voice in my life but nothing that pointed me to an answer to a question. In my life, the way God has spoken to me most often is through His Word, the Bible. In it, He gives me answers for questions about what He wants me to do. He gives me examples of behavior to follow. I don't have to ask, "What would Jesus do?" I can simply read about what Jesus did. So, I did. I read about Job and his trials and all the help he didn't get from his friends and his wife. I read about the man who cried out to Jesus, "I believe, Lord. Help my unbelief." I read about Simon carrying the cross of Jesus and about Aaron and Hur helping Moses keep his arms upraised during the battle with the Amalekites. I read all of these stories. They were great stories, but I needed to know about asking questions.

Then I read about John the Baptist. And I saw his story with new eyes. I saw John leap in his mother's womb at the presence of his cousin, the Christ. I saw John baptize Jesus and declare Him to be the Lamb that takes away sins. And I saw John in prison. I saw him send some of his followers to ask Jesus a question. I saw John, feeling the pressure of his persecution for teaching the gospel of Jesus, want answers. I saw Jesus when John's followers told the Christ that John wanted to know if Jesus was really the one to follow or if there was someone else coming. I saw Jesus tell John's followers to tell John about the miracles Jesus was doing. I saw Jesus tell people after John had this question about the very nature of Jesus, that there was not a greater man born of woman than John the Baptist. Jesus didn't get angry at the sincere question of a man hurting and wanting to be lifted up by the words of the Christ. John's sincere question did nothing to remove Jesus from His throne. My sincere question would not and will not do anything to detract from the worthiness and righteousness of Jesus.

So I asked questions. And I searched God's Word. And I put my face on the carpet of a quiet room and sought answers from God. And while I read those stories of Simon carrying Christ's cross and Aaron and Hur holding up Moses's arms, I saw them differently and realized that when the burden is too much, God puts *Simons* on our path to help us with our burden. I knew that other people had belief but needed help with their unbelief. I read Psalm 23 and knew that God had never promised me that I would walk around the valley of the shadow of death but that when I walked through it, He would walk with me. And I saw that Isaiah told me that I would stand in deep water and even fire but that God would stand with me. I read the story of how much God did not want His people to have a king but that God removed his hand of guidance from them and allowed them to have what they wanted despite His will. And I saw that when we leave God's will, bad will happen and affect others as well. I learned so much from God's Word after I asked God questions and let Him open my eyes to verses and stories that I had read before but now saw through eyes opened by Him. God is not afraid of our hurts and our fears and our questions. He already knows that we have them. We need to be honest with Him and ourselves and bare our hearts to Him so that He can heal us. My son is no less separated from me now than he was the night he died. It still hurts. But now I know that when the burden is too much for me to bear, God wants me to let Him take care of it.[5]

Journal

Session 3

Be Not Paralyzed

I was amazed one morning while reading my devotions. There
was question after question that Jesus asked specific people.
It was astonishing because the questions came from several
different devotionals and Bible passages. I gradually realized
Jesus was talking to me through each question He asked.
It became a very personal worship time in which I found
myself trying to answer each question from my heart.[1]

The Spirit of the Lord is upon me (the Messiah), because he has
anointed me to preach the good news to the poor. He has sent me to
announce release (pardon, forgiveness) to the captives, and recovery of
sight to the blind, to set free those who are oppressed (downtrodden,
bruised, crushed by tragedy), to proclaim the favorable year of the
Lord (the day when salvation and the favor of God abound greatly).
—Luke 4:18–19 (AMP)

Since you are taking this Bible study on grief, it is possible you have felt the effects of grief and have become immobilized. Paralyzed. There is no strength to move, to live, to carry out normal, everyday tasks that used to come so easily. Suddenly, your whole world has changed. Your outlook is different. Your faith is tested. How can we survive this loss when we are struggling to even function? When we are in deep grief, it is hard to imagine making it through another day, another moment. Our sorrow consumes us in our thoughts and actions.

The questions of Jesus have touched on so much of my grief in the areas of tears, fear, doubt, faith, and my relationship to the Lord. I was experiencing a paralyzation, if you will, that was troubling my soul. I had questions. I wanted answers. How could I move ahead until I could somehow grasp all I was experiencing? Besides all this, what about the areas of denial, anger, depression, bitterness, and bargaining with God? If we are not careful in these areas, we are in danger of staying too long. They can wreak destruction in our lives. That is why we must seek the Lord for His help. Sometimes His help involves using doctors. Do not rule this out. There are Christian doctors who are willing and able to counsel and assist with your need.

Jesus, our great Physician, is always available to us. He is our greatest need and our supreme help. Living through a tragedy allowed me to recognize this more clearly than I ever had up to that time. My neediness caused me to depend upon Him. I am praying that through this study, someone will be set free from a paralyzing effect of grief through our Lord Jesus Christ.

In Luke 4:18–19, Jesus is in the synagogue reading from Isaiah 61:1–2 and applying these verses to Himself, saying, "Today this scripture is fulfilled in your hearing" (verse 21). By saying this, Jesus is stating that the measureless gifts of the Spirit of the Lord are on Him. He has everything!

He was to preach *good news to the poor.* The good news is the gospel, and in preaching the gospel, *release (pardon, forgiveness) to the captives.* The gospel message is: Jesus came into the world to die for our sins, He was buried and rose again, and all who put their faith and trust in Him will be saved. Perhaps you are reading this and have never made a commitment to Christ, but you see your great need of Him in your life. We are all slaves to sin until we allow Jesus to be Lord of our lives and accept the forgiveness He offers through the cross. We must repent of our sins and receive Christ as our Lord. He loves you and gave Himself for you so that you could know Him. He so longs for you to come to Him, and all you have to do is repent of your sins and ask Him to come into your life. Salvation cost God everything, but He offers it to us freely. If you need Jesus, please ask Him now to come into your life. "Today, if you hear his voice, do not harden your hearts" (Hebrews 3:7–8a).

He preached *recovery of sight to the blind* by opening eyes to truth. Jesus is truth and light. He said, "I have come into the world as a light, so that no one who believes in me should stay in darkness" (John 12:46).

And, *to set free those who are oppressed (downtrodden, bruised, crushed by tragedy).* This is where we are going to settle down in the study.

Downtrodden—without hope, suffering oppression.

Bruised—to inflict psychological hurt.

Crushed by tragedy—to be pressed so hard, to the breaking point, to be overwhelmed by an event that causes great sadness and often involves someone's death.

How significant is it to you that Jesus wants to free you from hopelessness and help with overwhelming circumstances created from your loss?

_____

_____

_____

_____

Out of His great love for us, Jesus "took up our infirmities and carried our sorrows." "He was pierced for our transgressions, he was crushed for our iniquities" (Isaiah 53:4a and 5a). He was oppressed, bruised, unjustly accused, spat upon, and suffered and died for you and me, your sins and mine, and our guilt. This was the greatest darkness ever experienced by anyone. So, He is able to bring life to you. He understands your pain. He suffered so that we might have peace in our storms. We should lift up prayers of thanksgiving to Christ for being oppressed for our sake and crushed because of our sins. What other God would take your sins and give you His righteousness? No other! Second Corinthians 5:21 says, "God made him who had no sin to be sin for us, so that in him we might become the righteousness of God." Amazing!

Although I live with grief, I have accepted my loss in that I can't change my circumstances, and Jesus has given me life again through the tragedy and in the sadness. He has given me hope for now and a future hope of heaven, being with my son again, forever. Acceptance is freeing. Knowing we can't change our circumstances but learning to live in them is part of the progression of grief.

Child of God, why are you crying? In John 20:15, Jesus asked Mary Magdalene why she was crying. She was mourning, grieving at His tomb. But Jesus's body was not there. He had risen! I have found going to the cemetery peaceful. I'm sure not everyone feels this way, but it gives me a quiet time to reflect. The cemetery tells me that death is as much a part of life as living. Unless Jesus returns first, we will all experience death. Take encouragement from this verse in Psalm 49:15, "But God will redeem my life from the grave; he will surely take me to himself." Another version says it this way, "But God will reach into the grave and save my life from its power. He will fetch me and take me into His eternal house" (VOICE). I have stood many times at my son's grave and wept for him. It is out of love and devotion to those we've lost that we linger by their places of rest. Somehow it is a comfort to think we are close to our beloved one's body.

Listen, our tears can turn to joy because of Christ's resurrection. This is our hope. "For in this hope we are saved" (Romans 8:24). "Do not let your heart be troubled (afraid, cowardly). Believe (confidently) in God and trust in Him, (have faith, hold on to it, rely on it, keep going and) believe also in Me. In My Father's house are many dwelling places. If it were not so, I would have told you, because I am going there to prepare a place for you" (John 14:1–2 AMP).

So maybe that is why Jesus asked Mary why she was crying—for her to realize she could be rejoicing. Tears are cleansing. Sometimes after a good cry we see things clearer. Jesus opened her eyes to see that it was indeed He. "Jesus said to her, 'Mary'" (John 20:16). Oh, thank you, Jesus, that You know us so intimately and care for us so compassionately. Jesus says to me, "_____" (your name). How beautifully personal!

The very next sentence in John 20:16 says, "She turned toward him." Mary's focus since her new life with Christ had been fixed. He was her life. Our lives should be no less. Our focus and everything we do should be to glorify God. Focusing on Christ keeps us from being crushed. He knows our tears and one day will wipe them away.

"Why are you so afraid?" (Matthew 8:26). Fear can be a paralyzing emotion. When it pertains to grief and loss, fear can come in the form of helplessness, torturing thoughts, and new depths of emotions and feelings we had no knowledge of before. It may be because of this unknown journey we are embarking on or fearing for the one we have lost. And the list could go on.

Share a fear you have experienced because of your grief and loss.

_____

_____

_____

My fear was for my son. What did he have to suffer before death? I feared that he had feared, and I wouldn't want him to fear! Even though he is a Christian and I know Christians go to heaven, I needed to know from God that he was in fact there and was being cared for.

In Matthew 8:23–27, we are told the disciples and Jesus are in the boat when "a furious storm came up on the lake." My commentary says the storm was for the disciples' sakes, to show them to expect storms in this life that would test their faith. All the while, Jesus is in the back of the boat, asleep. How could Jesus sleep through rough waves, a rocking boat, and yelling disciples? By having total and complete trust in God the Father. He had no fear. The disciples, on the other hand, were in a panic and scared they would drown, so they woke Jesus up for help. Yes, we cry out to God for help when we are in fearful situations. Fear should drive us to God for deliverance. But Jesus's reply to them amazes me, "You of little faith, why are you so afraid?" In His compassion, Jesus is telling them they need not be fearful. We need not be fearful, O child of the living God! He has us under His wings, where we find refuge (Psalm 91:4).

More than me not wanting my son to have had fear, our heavenly Father doesn't want us to fear either. He wants us to be assured we are being taken care of in ways unimaginable to us, even in our suffering.

"Why did you doubt?" (Matthew 14:31). We use the word *doubt* so casually when in actuality it is a powerful word. It means distrust, uncertainty, suspicion, and unbelief.

Once again, the disciples are in a boat when a wind comes up. This time, Jesus is not with them. He sent them in the boat while He went up on a mountainside, alone, to pray. I would imagine the disciples were even more fearful this time because Jesus was not with them to help. Perhaps the Lord was testing their faith. During the first storm, He was close by, and now they had no idea where He was. Could they still trust Him to come to their rescue?

I can't help but think how differently their situation would have turned out if they had followed Jesus to the mountainside and spent most of the night praying with Him. Would they have been as fearful? "Do not be anxious about anything, but in everything, by prayer and petition, with thanksgiving, present your requests to God. And the peace of God, which transcends all understanding, will guard your hearts and your minds in Christ Jesus" (Philippians 4:6–7).

How essential is it to your faith to trust when you cannot see God working, understand your circumstances, or sense His love and watch care over you?

_____

_____

Jesus came to their rescue in a way they would have never dreamed: walking on water, and it terrified them (Matthew 13:26). Oh, the sovereignty of Christ! He can rescue us any way He chooses. He said to them, "Take courage!" It takes courage to grow our faith. Peter is our example of this as he says to the Lord, "If it's you, tell me to come to you on the water." And Jesus said, "Come." And for a moment, Peter was brave and believed—until he took his eyes off the Lord and focused on the wind and waves. Then he began to sink. However, Peter had witnessed the previous storm stop at Jesus's command, so he cried out, "Lord, save me!" Remembering God's faithfulness in the past will help grow our faith for the future. Peter knew what to do, but don't you know that when the Lord said to him, "You of little faith, why did you doubt?" he was overcome with sorrow for not believing?

What is causing doubt? Have your eyes focused on your storm and not on Jesus? Jesus says, "Come." See how much He loves you. Step out into faith with Him. I know that I don't want to sink in doubt. I want to say, "Increase my faith!" (Luke 17:5). Then, whether He calms the storm raging in your life or calms the storm in your soul, give Him the praise and glory. "Truly you are the Son of God" (Matthew 14:33).

"And why do you worry?" (Matthew 6:28a). In the following verses, Jesus says, "Do not worry" several times. It is so hard to follow this command. Our concerns are real. Some are life altering, and we progress from concern to worry quickly. We especially do this if the subjects of concern are our children or spouses. Our thoughts become confused as we conjure up scenarios that may never happen. In these verses, Jesus is talking mainly about our basic needs: food and clothes, those "worries of this life" that Jesus was talking about in the parable of the sower (Mark 9:19). These worries choke out God, His voice, and His Word and turn our eyes inward to our problems. We try to fix what's causing the worry instead of going to God and believing what He said, "Do not worry."

Because we live in a fallen world, the temptation to worry is ongoing. The remedy for worry is in 1 Peter 5:7, "Cast all your anxiety on him because he cares for you." I should fix my thoughts on Christ and His words about worrying, instead of the crisis at hand. Jesus asks, "Who of you by worrying can add a single hour to his life?" (Matthew 6:27). Worrying didn't change my circumstances. Worrying doesn't change circumstances.

God is able to meet every need we could possibly have! The problem is we do not always do what He asks in order to have those needs met. "Seek first his kingdom and his righteousness, and all these things will be given to you as well" (Matthew 6:33). He is willing and able to take care of all our needs if we trust Him. These verses in Matthew are so simple to understand yet hard to live out, but Jesus makes it very clear that we are not to worry. Jesus said in John 14:1, "Do not let your hearts be troubled. Trust in God, trust also in me." God will not keep us from worrying. It is an act of will on our part to believe and trust.

Grief counselors talk about the passage of grief and the danger of being paralyzed in one place too long. Let's look at this, and if you feel you cannot find a way to move forward, you may want to consider Christian counseling.

Denial. When my son's accident happened and for several months afterward, I had a hard time comprehending he was gone. I was in shock and felt I was living a nightmare. I would think he was going to call or come home and then have to remind myself of the reality that he was never going to be here again. A part of me wanted to believe he was here, but I also realized how much I needed to grasp the truth. This was my new way of life—not what I would have chosen but nonetheless reality. I can't say I was ever in true denial, but I easily understood why anyone struggling with such a tragic loss would want to go into a thought process of nonacceptance to hide from the pain.

Anger. I struggled with being angry toward God. Why would He take my child, my only child, when He could have prevented the accident? In His great mercy and loving, compassionate grace, He walked me through the anger, and I am grateful that He understood my heart and my hurt. However, others may struggle with anger from a different viewpoint. Perhaps anger rises because someone was responsible for the loss. What a difficult situation to work out. Remember, God's grace is sufficient no matter what the circumstance. Nothing is too hard for the Lord. Pour your heart out to Him. Perhaps you didn't find the help you needed in an illness. It could be that there is anger toward the person who has died, in the case of suicide, or anger with oneself. Whatever the cause of the anger, getting it resolved will free your heart and mind. And I might add, with God's help, forgiveness may be in order. Forgiveness is freeing. If you are dealing with how to forgive or whether you should forgive, think about the unconditional love and grace our Lord has shown us, even when we didn't deserve it.

Depression. We will clearly plunge into depression from our circumstances every now and again. Knowing what we have lost, what could have been but will never be, is a sadness we revisit many times over. When I see it in myself, I'm okay with it for a few days, but I realize I can't stay there. As much as I would like to, I can't isolate myself from the world, because I know it isn't emotionally healthy.

Bargaining. My dad told me that he tried to bargain with God shortly after his grandson's passing. He could not bear the pain from losing his only grandson and watching his daughter suffer at the same time. He asked God to let Gary live and take him, if God would just change the circumstances.

Bitterness/cynicism. I'm not a counselor, but I believe bitterness takes root when we dwell too long and wallow in our sorrow, anger, depression, and denial. Bitterness will eat away at you like a poison and truly needs to be worked through. I found myself being cynical early in my grief. I remember a time when someone was overly upset over a trivial issue, and I wanted to scream, "Really? My son just died, and you are upset over something so small?" I have had to watch myself with this from time to time. Death of a loved one tends to give life perspective, and the small things do not affect me like they used to. However, I need to be aware of the fact that others may not have suffered through a life-altering tragedy, and their issues are important to them. Bitterness can easily worm its way into our lives when we can't understand why God has permitted the circumstance that has left us in such heartache.

Be watchful of the bitterness, the doubt (unbelief), the worry, the anger, and the fear that can rise up in life. Our enemy can use these against us. Be alert and make the choice to trust your heavenly Father, the one who loves you and cares about everything you are going through. It is freeing to know that God is in control and is constant over your life. The key is to remain in the vine (John 15), for without Him, we can do nothing.

There are two stories at the end of this session. Rosemary's story addresses the aftermath of the suicide of her son. One of her struggles was blaming herself and how she works through that. The amazing part is how she was able to keep praising God even in the midst of her pain. Her story will inspire others who sadly are experiencing the loss of a loved one through suicide.

Gary's story is one of brutal murder and torture of his daughter. Hate, rage, and vengeance permeated his life. His story will show how our awesome God can restore such a man. Gary's story will compel you to seek out Jesus for the peace of mind and heart you are yearning to possess, and allow God's grace to bring you to a place where you can forgive someone for even the most heinous act.

We must allow ourselves time to grieve. This is a time of change. Our whole life has been upset. Processing all the new emotions, thoughts, and everything pertaining to our new way of life takes time. I have been on this journey several years now, and I still have times of hard grieving. I realize I always will, and that is acceptable to me. I do not want to forget. Grief is a process that won't end until I go home to heaven. I want to grieve in a positive way in the midst of living life, while I'm learning to live with my loss. First Thessalonians 4:13b says, "Do not grieve like the rest of mankind, who have no hope." I want to know God in a more intimate way because of my loss. Even in my sorrow, He has blessed me beyond measure. I am thankful for the opportunities to serve Him because of my loss. If I had been paralyzed by any emotion from grief, unable to move forward for long periods of time, I would not have grown in my Christian walk. Grief, if given to God, builds our trust in Him and our character as Christians. It inspires us and drives us to ministry. Where would I be now had I not believed God's Word and stood on His promises? It scares me to think of my life without God. My sorrow and loss have deepened my love, my heart, and my compassion toward other sufferers. And it has strengthened my love for the Lord. He is still working on me. I am a work in progress, but the key word is *progress*.

As much as I love to read and learn, I've noticed that the grief I have experienced plays on my memory. The fact that I'm growing older, the stresses of life, and too much to do add to my thinking process as well. That's why I've found that writing down times when God has shown me evidence of Him in my life and in my thoughts is essential; otherwise, I might forget those times. I need to be reminded daily of His guidance and love. If I don't have these reminders, it leaves open the capacity to lose faith and the endurance to move on. Remembering is biblical. Throughout the

Bible, God asked His people to remember what He had done for them in the past. On another note, we can ask God to remember His promises to us, not that He needs reminding, but it helps us to recall in our minds all His good promises.

God's grace will see you through, dear one. Trust Him to help you move forward and grow your character to glorify Him in and because of your sorrow and loss. Afflictions are not meant to paralyze us for the rest of our lives but are meant to help us draw closer to the Lord. Jesus asked the blind man who was calling out and begging Him to listen, "What do you want me to do for you?" (Luke 18:41). What is it you need from our Lord today? He is tenderly waiting for you to "come." Let Him set you free from being paralyzed.

Record this promise from Psalm 119:75–77

_____

_____

_____

The Message Bible says it this way: "your testing has taught me what's true and right. Oh, love me—and right now!—hold me tight! Just the way you promised. Now comfort me so I can live, really live."

God's Faithful Personal Promise

Write out Psalm 9:9–10

_____

_____

_____

Isaiah 42:3 and quoted again in Matthew 12:20

_____

_____

_____

Psalm 34:18

_____

_____

2 Peter 1

_____

_____

_____

Oh, grieving one, the more we come to know God as our refuge and see Him working on our behalf, the more we will grow in our faith. He will tend to us and mend our broken hearts and will not allow us to be crushed or consumed by the weight of our grief. He is our stronghold and our strength!

Journal Quote:

> Grief changes everyone. We either embrace the hard work of grief and learn the lessons it brings, or we become slaves on its ravaged plains of despair. We are responsible for owning our grief, seeing it for what it is, but inviting it to change us, deepen us, and grow our souls. It is the only sure road to restoration.[2] (Susan Duke, *Grieving Forward*)

Rosemary's Story

It was a nice summer day, June 23, 2017, to be exact, when all our belongings were packed and we were moving to Walland, Tennessee, from Denver, Colorado. At least we were planning to pack the truck that day. The movers were on their way over, and we were scheduled to pick up a large truck at noon. While walking the dogs that morning, I fell. I knew I was hurt but slowly tried to get up and see just how badly. It was pretty evident that my ribs were hurting, and my first thought was that I had fractured some of them. It turned out they were only bruised, though painful nonetheless.

We left before noon to pick up the truck, and when we got there, they told us that some sort of problem had occurred and the truck was being worked on. It wouldn't be until later that day that the truck would be ready for pickup. However, they said, "We're sure you will get everything into this sixteen-foot truck." We had ordered a twenty-six-foot truck but assumed they knew what they were talking about, so we might as well try it. So, home we went with the sixteen-foot truck. The movers basically laughed at us after looking at our apartment and seeing all the furniture and boxes we had. They told us they couldn't possibly get everything in that small truck and weren't even going to try. Plus, they had another job to go to. We immediately got on the phone and in no uncertain terms let the trucking company know that we had had the truck reserved for two months and weren't listening to any more of their excuses. By 4:00 p.m. that afternoon, we had the truck we had first requested delivered to our apartment. By this time, the movers had gone on to their other job; they would be back Sunday morning to finish the job.

It was long and arduous, but we got out of town Monday as planned. We made the long trip, with my husband driving the truck and my niece from Colorado driving our car with our two dogs and me as her passengers. We spent one night outside of St. Louis and arrived at our destination the next day.

In the next two months, we got everything unpacked, hung pictures, started painting our kitchen cupboards a pretty gray, finished the doors with new silver hardware, and started enjoying life in Tennessee.

My sister knew we were going grocery shopping that fateful afternoon of August 23, 2017, so she called and asked if we'd left for the store yet. I told her we were just leaving. She asked us to stop by her place first. We tried to change that stop until after we got our groceries, but she wouldn't have any of that, so we acquiesced and went to her place as she requested. When we walked in, everyone was somber-faced, and we knew something was wrong. She asked us to sit down and proceeded to tell me that my son, Eric, had died. I went into shock and started crying. I asked how he died and if it was in his own plane that he had built. They said they didn't know but that the county sheriff would be coming to give all of us the details. My daughter in Ft. Collins, Colorado, had arranged to have that done because she didn't want anyone to misconstrue the details.

Just before the sheriff knocked at the door, I remarked that I surely hoped it wasn't by suicide, knowing it couldn't possibly have been. When he came in, he sat down and didn't waste any time giving us the horrible news that my son had, indeed, committed suicide by strangulation. I burst out with the most awful cry and couldn't believe my ears. It felt like I was watching a movie but knew it wasn't real, so it would be okay. It didn't sink in, and I couldn't wrap my mind around what we had just been told. It was surreal. I didn't know what going into shock meant until I tried to call my niece in Phoenix from the living room of my sister's house and couldn't find my way back to the sunroom. Then on the way home, I asked my husband if he had taken a different route, because none of the houses or roads looked familiar. *That night changed my life forever.*

After we got home that night and I went to bed, I couldn't stop praising the Lord and even thanking Him. This was unbelievable to me that I could do that after hearing this horrific news about my son. But isn't this what He tells us to do? Little did I know that I could actually do it. Oh, but wait, it wasn't me who did it but the Holy Spirit within me that held it all together and allowed me to praise and thank the Lord. I wasn't thanking Him for what happened to my son but *in spite* of what happened to my son. I knew Jesus protected me from going off the deep end. He was right there with me with His arms tightly around me, and it was as if I could actually feel it. He never left my side during that awful, shock-filled night. He even put me to sleep and gave me a restful night.

It wasn't that night that this verse came to me, but now when I hear it or read it in the Word, it makes me know, more fully, the truth of what I must have felt that night and to this very day. Ephesians 3:16–19 says, "I pray that out of His glorious riches He may strengthen you with power through His Spirit in your inner being, so that Christ may dwell in your hearts through faith. And I pray that you, being rooted and established in love, may have power, together with all the saints, to grasp how wide and long and high and deep is the love of Christ, and to know this love that surpasses knowledge—that you may be filled to the measure of all the fullness of God."

My son, Eric, was fifty years old when he died. He left a son, Tucker, who was to turn twenty-one within the next month, a wife, a mother, and two sisters. His father had passed away years before. He had also served in the Air National Guard and spent some time in Iraq, Oman, and

Afghanistan. He didn't seem to be quite the same when he returned. He had gotten somewhat bitter with everyone. He and I had our times when things weren't as good and we weren't as close as I would have liked us to be, but we were just getting back to being friends again, and I prayed so fervently night after night that he and I would be as close as we once were.

The following days and weeks after Eric's death, I knew for certain it was all my fault (in my own mind). I had taken his and his sister's daddy away from them when Eric was five and Wendy was nine, through divorce. No little girl or boy should have to grow up without a parent, unless God decides to take one of them home. It was confusing to both of them, and due to my having to work for a living for the first time, they were alone a lot. When I let myself think about this, even to this day, it still makes me very sad, and I feel deep remorse for this selfish act. I steeped myself in the Word and in my devotion time every morning and every evening before turning the light out. It is still difficult for me to think I had nothing to do with his death, but the Lord has shown me Himself in many ways: through peace that surpasses all human knowledge, His loving me in spite of myself, leading me to many godly writers who write wonderful devotional material, reading His Word every day without fail, support through my church family, and a loving relationship with my two daughters and other family members. I would like to be able to tell you that I *never* believe Satan's lies anymore about how unworthy I am, and that my sin is too great to be forgiven, but when I allow him to do that, the Holy Spirit reminds me that God frees us to receive His love and know the joy of forgiveness.

Two months after Eric's death, I had an accident near the University of Tennessee. I did about $10,000 worth of damage to our car, and the young man I rear-ended had one little puncture by the bolt on his license plate. Two months after that, we had to put our sixteen-year-old dog to sleep, and two months after that, just recently, we had to totally replace our HVAC system. You think we didn't and still don't wonder if our move to Tennessee was the thing we were supposed to do and was God-directed?

When I felt, and still feel sometimes, like a lot of my life has been spent in the desert, with no trees, no water, no animals, and no food, I came upon this Bible verse that I now have claimed for myself: "Though the fig tree does not bud and there are no grapes on the vines, though the olive crop fails and the fields produce no food, though there are no sheep in the pen and no cattle in the stalls, YET I will rejoice in the Lord. I will be joyful in God my Savior" (Habakkuk 3:17–18).[3]

Gary's Story

Note: Gary's story of his courtroom battles was televised. The world watched while this man rocked back and forth with hatred and anger filling his eyes and heart. I personally have witnessed his transformation and how he now uses his story to bring others to a saving knowledge of Jesus Christ through the loss and heartache he endures.

In January 2007, the murders of Channon Christian and Christopher Newsom rocked the city of Knoxville, Tennessee. I lived every parent's worst nightmare.

Every day, I got on my knees and asked God to protect my children. When Channon was tortured, raped, and murdered, I turned away from God. I told Him I was done with Him. I lived the next eight years full of hate, anger, and revenge. I spend 398 days in hearings and trials. There were seven capital murder trials total. In the process, the judge was arrested for drug abuse and two of the defendants got more trials. Both families sat day after day, week after week, having to listen to one lie after another about our children. We could not show emotion, we could not cry, we could not show anger, all because they did not want us to improperly influence the jury. I wanted nothing more than to kill the five animals responsible for my baby girl's death. I spent a great deal of time trying to forgive and figure out just how to accomplish that goal.

In 2017 on Easter Sunday, I was coaxed into going to church with some of my club members. The second I walked into the church, I wanted to leave. God started working on me the second the preacher started his message. The similarities of Christ's brutal death on the cross and all the torture reminded me of the abuse Channon endured.

The preacher talked about Peter and how he had turned his back on God and how after Christ came out of the tomb, He restored Peter back to where he was before he denied Christ.

Peter and I had a lot in common: turning our backs on God.

A couple of weeks later, I went back to the same church, and the same pastor talked about how the justice system was broken and how we would never get justice in this world.

I met my club members at Channon's grave to honor our memorial motorcycle ride. When I got there and we all gathered around Channon's grave, I realized I was so tired of fighting the evil in this world by myself. I just could not fight anymore. I went down on my knees and asked Christ to restore me just as He did with Peter. Then I asked Him to please use me to make a difference in this world. Christ restored me that second, like He had been waiting on me to come home all along.

God has given me a huge platform with many stories to tell, with the biggest one the story of how Christ restored a man who had completely turned his back on Him for many years, and that no matter how deep and dark the abyss you have climbed into, no matter how dark your life has become, Christ can and will restore you and will restore your witness and use you for His glory and His kingdom in a mighty way.[4]

Journal

Session 4

Lost and Separated

You keep track of all my sorrows.
You have collected all my tears in your bottle.
You have recorded each one in your book.
—Psalm 56:8 (NLT)

This has been a hard lesson for me to write. It was a fresh and still vivid experience that led to this subject of feeling lost and separated. Even though I have lived with grief for several years now, one of God's creatures recently brought out the illustration I will share in this session. This is a tough subject, but it is a very real part of grief.

Hate is a strong word. When it comes to losing loved ones, I hate death! I hate loss! I hate separation! The anxiety separation brings is overwhelming. It is a lost and lonely feeling. It is absolute mental agony. My child is part of me, my flesh, my heart, and this part is gone, and there is nothing I can do to bring my son back. It is a helpless frustration that is out of my control.

God understands. He knows those feelings. He has already suffered a separation. And He endured it out of love for us, so He is able to give comfort. He didn't say He would take our grief away. He did say He is always with us. He will reassure us and will hold, even carry, us when we feel we can't go on. He records every tear.

Why do you think God would record every tear?

_____

_____

_____

When David wrote Psalms 55 and 56, he was in dire straits with the enemy. David was sure that God was on his side, working for his deliverance. Even in the midst of his fear and distress, David cried out to God for help, for comfort, for mercy, and he knew that God heard his pleas. "Evening, morning and noon I cry out in distress, and he hears my voice" (Psalm 55:17). I know this is what God wants us to do in our sorrows and loss. Confide in and talk to Him. Tell Him about your heartache and trust that He hears you and will come to minister to you. God is on your side. "Blessed are those who mourn, for they will be comforted" (Matthew 5:4).

My illustration -

Early one Sunday morning I was having coffee on our back porch. Behind our house, beyond our yard, is farmland and cattle. In the distance, I could hear the farmer calling in the cows. They were mooing. I thought maybe he was bringing them a roll of hay to eat, but that wasn't it at all. In just a little while, the farmers truck and cattle trailer went by our house with a mooing cow inside. At the time, I didn't think much about it. Not until the next day, and the next, and the next. For in the field beyond our yard, was a mother cow, pacing, bawling, and calling for her calf. When at first, I heard her, the realization came of what had happened the day before: The farmer had taken her calf away. Every day she was out looking for him. I listened to her hooves pounding the ground as she walked back and forth in the field calling her calf. She wanted her baby! Where was he? What happened to him? The separation from her calf drove her to look aimlessly everywhere, calling for him for a week! And she is a cow! My heart seemed to explode and I burst into tears, irrepressible tears! Standing in my back yard, I looked up to heaven and cried out to God, "I hate the separation!"

If you feel you can, put into words what you are encountering from the experience of separation.

_____

_____

_____

Sometimes we go over and over the circumstances that brought about the loss of our loved ones. Whether you had to witness your loved one depart slowly from an illness or suddenly from a tragic accident, we all have a memory of that time we are working through. To be very transparent with you, my mind travels under water where I see my son drowning. I hate that word—*drown*. I can't bear the sight in my mind, so why do I go there? Because I wonder about my child, what was going through his mind when the desperation of needing to breathe overcame him. When he realized he wasn't going to make it to the surface. This is pure torture and a reality I live with.

I've heard people say, "God spared my loved one and protected them from death. God was with them." Yes, He was. However, God was with my son too. I am confident of this, and perhaps even angels were right by his side and comforted him. He was never left alone, not for one second. God is always with us, and that is a promise. Just like David in the two Psalms, when he was in the greatest danger and had the most fear, he knew who to call to for help. He knew who his deliverer was. This is the same God. This is our God. He never changes.

Describe the comfort knowing that God was with your believing loved one, especially at the moment of death.

_____

_____

_____

I'm finding that it takes much courage to mourn, and it takes time. We need to have times of grieving and mourning. We need time to be with *others* and time to be by *ourselves*. Our friends can help carry us along. They encourage us with their presence. They get us out and away from the grief that is consuming us and teach us that life is still going on. They help us to know that eventually we will rejoin the living, but we will rejoin with new perspectives, new compassions, and new God-given strength. Yes, we need others in our lives. We also need time to ourselves. Time to contemplate. Time to learn how to live with our grief. And we need rest because grief is exhausting.

God doesn't want you to stay alone and grieve constantly. Staying too long creates despair and depression. It takes an effort of will to be motivated and pull away and come back to life. The Lord will help you endure. He is the only true source of hope. God can set your feet on a rock and give you a firm place to stand (Psalm 40:2).

There are lessons to be taught in the school of grief that can never be learned any other way. Keep your heart open to what God is teaching you about Himself. Sorrow has enriched the lives of others throughout history. When we choose to believe that God can take our sorrow and weave it into our character for His glory, we will come out stronger. We will be more compassionate for other sufferers. The act of choosing can place us on a path to healing, learning, and growing in our walk with the Lord. We have a choice to stay in the darkness of despair, or we can take hold of the light of the world, Jesus (John 8:12).

In Brandi's story at the end of this session, she chose to praise her Lord even through the tragic loss of her son. Through the words of a song he had sung, she took hold of them and found her strength.

I have this keen sense that this separation is only temporary. Up ahead, I can see a reunion coming on. I'm thankful our son isn't sitting around grieving for us as we do for him. It is freeing to know he is busy worshipping, serving, praising, and working for the Lord. He is completely happy and content. When I allow my mind to think on the truths from scripture, I start seeing progression in my grief. I become more positive in my outlook. I feel better than I did several years ago about my loss and the separation because I have believed in the promises of God. The most tragic separation would be separation from God. Then, there is no hope. But we are not of those who have no hope. We are of those who believe (1 Timothy 4:10)!

In John 16:20, we find Jesus explaining to his puzzled disciples about His imminent death. He tells them they will grieve, but their grief will turn to joy. He was assuring them of a return of joy in a future day. He was giving them hope and a great promise to look forward to. This joy will one day be ours when we see our believing loved ones again, and it will be sweet joy. "Weeping may remain for a night, but rejoicing comes in the morning" (Psalm 30:5b). Another version says it this way: "The nights of crying your eyes out give way to days of laughter" (MSG).

Bishop Ryle from the nineteenth century wrote, "Those whom you laid in the grave with many tears are in good keeping: you will see them again with joy. Believe it, think it, rest on it. It is all true."[1]

"Listen, I tell you a mystery: We will not sleep, but we will all be changed—in a flash, in the twinkling of an eye, at the last trumpet. For the trumpet will sound, the dead will be raised imperishable, and we will be changed. … Therefore … stand firm. Let nothing move you"

(1 Corinthians 15:51–52, 58).

Read and think on these four scriptures passages: Philippians 1:20–23, 1 Corinthians 15:42–44, 1 Thessalonians 4:13–18, and Romans 8:38–39.

Write out the one that encourages your heart today.

_____

_____

_____

If our grief is being directed in a way that grows our faith instead of leaving us in despair, we are traveling in the right direction on this journey. Let your sorrow deepen you. Mourning for those we've lost causes us to think more, search for God more, and live stronger. Be valiant!

I choose for my grief to grow me closer to God, so I will seek Him out, from His Word and in prayer. I will watch for Him in life and see where and how He may be working. I will offer up my grief to be used for His purposes. I will wait in hope.

God's Faithful Personal Promise

Write out Habakkuk 3:17–19.

_____

_____

_____

The Amplified Bible says of verse 19: "The Lord God is my Strength, my personal bravery, and my invincible army; He makes my feet like hinds' feet and will make me walk (not to stand still in terror, but to walk) and make (spiritual) progress upon my high places (of trouble, suffering, or responsibility)!" Amen!

Journal Passage:

> Blessed and greatly favored is the man whose strength is in You, in whose heart are the highways to Zion. Passing through the Valley of Weeping (Baca), they make it a place of springs.

> They go from strength to strength (increasing in victorious power).

> O LORD of hosts, How blessed and greatly favored is the man who trusts in You (believing in You, relying on You, and committing himself to You with confident hope and expectation). (Psalm 84:5–6a, 7a, 12 AMP)

Brandi's Story

One of the first songs that Chandler (my son) learned to play on the guitar was "Blessed Be Your Name." I can remember being at home, and he would play this song and sing. My two daughters and I would join right in. That memory brings a smile to my face.

I was driving to work last week; the date was June 21. This song came on while driving, and I hadn't heard it in so long. I don't think it was a coincidence. June 22 would be the third anniversary of Chandler's death.

Listening to the words, I began asking myself questions.

Am I still able to say the words, "Blessed be the name of the Lord"? Even in my loss? When I am walking in the desert? When the darkness is closing in around me? When there is great pain in the offering?

On June 22, 2013, I was dealt a blow that completely wiped me out. It brought me to the ground. It was just a normal Saturday. But it turned out to be the most devastating loss of my life. It was the day that we received the call that every parent dreads. The call that asks you to come to the hospital as soon as possible because your child is there injured. No details. Just come.

When we arrived, we were directed to an isolated room in the emergency department where everyone knows nothing good comes from those rooms. I have to say, looking back, I knew Chandler was gone. I didn't want to even think that and blocked it every second, but a mama's heart knows. While waiting for what seemed like an eternity, I began to hear the Lord speaking to my soul. He said, "Brandi, what the enemy means for evil, I mean for good. I am here with you right now. I am with Greg (my husband). But most importantly, I am with Chandler. Fall into Me. I will hold you up. You will need Me now." I cannot describe in words the grace that God extended to me that day. I could feel the grace from the second I walked through those hospital doors. I knew that, even in the commotion and chaos around me, God was there.

Then the physicians and a lot of other people came into the room. Three years later, I do not know what exactly they said to me. All I knew was that my son had accidentally shot himself in the head; the damage was too extensive, and he would not survive. They explained that he was on a ventilator to help him breathe. They were moving him to the ICU, and we could see him soon.

It wasn't very long until they took us to the ICU to see him. That was a walk that Greg and I took together. Hand in hand. I remember the sound of the machines breathing for him. I remember walking in and seeing him there. He was so peaceful. It looked like he was just sleeping. They pronounced him deceased around 7:20 that evening. We did not have to turn the ventilator off due to him being an organ donor.

The next few days, weeks, and months are still very blurry to me. The pain was and is excruciating. I have heard so many people say that no one should ever have to bury their child. That is the truest statement I have ever heard.

I had to go back to the verse that God had whispered over my soul that day.

"As for you, you meant evil against me, but God meant it for good in order to bring about this present result, to preserve many people alive" (Genesis 50:20 NASB).

I had to decide quickly what I believed to be true. I had to hold on to what I knew to be true. And that is my God is sovereign. Even when my circumstances did not turn out the way I thought they should. They did not change. For me, there was not another choice but to believe God's promises to me and that He would bring good out of this horrible tragedy.

He did. He still does. I see the good all the time. However, I have to be intentional to look for the good. Or I find myself just overcome with the bad. So far, I have seen salvation in many lives through the impact that Chandler had on the people around him. I have witnessed five lives saved through Chandler's choice to be an organ donor. Reading the verse above, His promise has been fulfilled to me. The verse says, "To preserve many people alive." I have seen lives given to the Lord, which leads to eternal life. I have seen lives redirected to paths that have them living out God's purpose for their lives.

Some days it's too hard, and I see myself giving up. It's so hard to long to parent a child that you can no longer see. And that longing is just as strong as it was the day Chandler left us. The pain takes my breath away. But the Lord gives me the grace to get up each day, bloody feet and all.

If you are reading this, you have experienced the devastating loss of losing your child or loved one. I urge you to step out in faith and believe the promises that God has given you through His Word. I am praying for each of you who have picked up this study to find the healing you are in desperate need of. May this be the day that healing begins. I pray that you come to a place where I and many others that you will read about in this book have come. We are able to say confidently through our pain, "Blessed be the name of the Lord."[2]

Journal

Session 5

The Journey Is Too Much for You

Digging out is hard. It takes effort. It takes will. Choosing
to dig out is the brave way. If I may be so bold, choosing
self-pity, despair, and bitterness is the coward's way.[1]

He (Elijah) came to a broom tree, sat down under it and prayed
that he might die. "I have had enough, LORD," he said. "Take
my life …" Then he lay down under the tree and fell asleep.
—1 Kings 19:4b–5a

The journey was too much for me. I had no strength, no will to
live. Life had been ripped right out of me. What was the point
of going on? Every hope and dream for my son instantly and
tragically vanished. There was no grasping this thought, no way for my
mind to comprehend this truth. What I wanted was to wake up from the
nightmare and realize it had all been a bad dream. But every time I woke
up from sleep, reality flooded my soul once again. *How can this be? What
will I do? Where do I go from here?*

Grief comes crashing into our lives. Nothing matters except the grief that engulfs us. There is no motivation, no resolve to escape.

Has your journey been too much for you to bear? Describe how.

_____

_____

_____

_____

I feel sure most of us have heard someone tell us, "God won't put on you more than you can bear." Or, "God never gives us more than we can handle." And we wonder why we cannot bear the grief that has overtaken us. These statements come from those who are trying to comfort and encourage us even though the passage they use to hold up this statement is actually regarding temptation, not suffering. It is 1 Corinthians 10:13, "No temptation has seized you except what is common to man. And God is faithful; he will not let you be tempted beyond what you can bear. But when you are tempted, he will also provide a way out so that you can stand up under it."

There is a way out of temptation. However, suffering is different.

When the journey becomes too much, everyone in the family is suffering. We all need the support and comfort from each other. Acknowledging our grief to each other is helpful and reassuring. On the other side, trying to spare us by ignoring the loss doesn't make it go away, and not mentioning the one we have lost is similar to stating that they never existed. This journey is wearisome and at times heavy laden. If this is the path you have been led to walk, take one step at a time. Sometimes it will seem you have taken one step forward and three steps backward, and you may feel burdened down. Depression is likely to overshadow us. This is a time to rest, and rest in the arms of Jesus.

Your soul will never be satisfied without God. "As the deer pants for streams of water, so my soul pants for you, O God. My soul thirsts for

God, for the living God" (Psalm 42:1–2). Our faith in God always needs to grow. Until we get to our heavenly home and our faith has sight, we should never be satisfied and stop growing. "Blessed are those who hunger and thirst for righteousness, for they will be filled" (Matthew 5:6). Perhaps you have been tested in your faith because of your afflictions. It could be that you are questioning whether God is even aware of you and your pain.

Be honest with God and yourself: where are you in your relationship with the Lord?

_____

_____

_____

_____

Elijah, that great prophet of God, had just been used of God to prove that He is the living God! And there is no other like Him (1 Kings 18). After this great miracle, "Elijah climbed to the top of Carmel, bent down to the ground and put his face between his knees" and prayed for rain (1 Kings 18:42). And it rained for the first time in years! This man had a relationship with the Lord!

The very next thing we see in scripture is Elijah scared and running for his life. What happened to that great prophet? What happened to the trust he showed for his Lord? He ran to Beersheba, left his servant there, and proceeded to go a day's journey into the desert (1 Kings 19:1–3). His fear took his eyes off God and instead focused on his circumstances. His circumstances led him to a depressed and discouraged state, and in weariness, he wanted to die. He had had enough. We are all capable of being in this condition. We get worn and tired of fighting all the different emotions that won't let our minds rest. The tears that flow wear us out and leave us exhausted. So, sleep, child of God, and rest. He is with you. "He makes me lie down in green pastures, he leads me beside quiet waters, he restores my soul" (Psalm 23:2–3a).

God doesn't want us to stay in this place of weariness. He helps us take the next step. "All at once an angel touched him and said, 'Get up and eat.' He looked around and there by his head was a cake of bread baked over hot coals, and a jar of water. He ate and drank and then lay down again" (1 Kings 19:5b–6). The simple things like eating and drinking to give us nourishment and strength are God-designed things to help us in our journey. Sleep heals our bodies and keeps them fighting. Finding a peaceful place to rest and reflect helps to restore our souls. "The angel of the Lord came back a second time and touched him and said, 'Get up and eat, for the journey is too much for you.' So he got up and ate and drank" (verses 7–8a).

Elijah had enough sustenance for his journey in moving forward. God will give you everything you need to continue on. Jesus taught his disciples to pray for their needs daily, "Give us this day our daily bread" (Matthew 6:11). He wants you to rely on Him always, especially when the journey is too much. He will provide.

In 2 Corinthians 1, Paul wrote to the church in Corinth about his sufferings and hardships. He said, "We were under great pressure, far beyond our ability to endure, so that we despaired even of life. Indeed, in our hearts we felt the sentence of death" (verse 8b). Although Paul is talking about being persecuted as a Christian, we can also apply this to our grief. I have been overwhelmed and did not think I could endure the pain I was suffering. I was immersed in heartache and felt I would die in my grief. I don't mean I've been suicidal. I have not. I'm implying my grief was so heavy I didn't know if I was going to be able to stand under the weight of it. But I found the resource to carrying on, relying on God. The very next thing Paul says is, "But this happened that we might not rely on ourselves but on God, who raises the dead" (verse 9). God may allow all other avenues for strength to fail in order for us to see our great need of Him.

What are some of the ways you might rely on God to carry you in your grief?

_____

_____

_____

This is the key: Jesus said, "Remain in me, and I will remain in you. No branch can bear fruit by itself; it must remain in the vine … apart from me you can do nothing" (John 15:4a and 5b). Our God is all-sufficient. You can rely on Him.

When Elijah arrived at the cave at Mount Horeb, "the word of the LORD came to him: 'what are you doing here, Elijah?'" (1 Kings 19:9). After, Elijah offered his complaint about everything that had taken place and, in his self-pity, appeared ready to give it all up. He was through. He was tired. What was the point of going on? Yet God gave him ears to hear a gentle whisper and told him things he was not aware of. God wasn't through with Elijah. God had a plan, and Elijah was wrong; he was not alone. God had stood by him and would stand by him and lead him forward. There were others that Elijah didn't know about who were faithful to God. And may it comfort us to know there are those around us who are also suffering in grief. We search for those to whom we can relate. Just like Elijah, we can continue in this journey and trust the One who is guiding our path.

Even if your journey has been a long one over several years, like the stories of Tammy and her daughter, Clara Ruth, at the end of this session, be confident the Lord will continue providing for you. Accepting each family member's different way of grieving is essential to the well-being of the home.

Are you ready to give it all up? Does the journey seem too much for you? Record these words of Jesus.

John 6:35 _____

_____

_____

Jesus told the disciples this just after they had witnessed the feeding of the five thousand. Jesus had taken the five loaves and miraculously made it enough to feed everyone and even had twelve baskets leftover! Take note: they had as much as they wanted! Jesus has our physical and spiritual needs covered if we will just allow him entrance into our lives.

John 4:10 _____

_____

_____

If we are in relationship with our Lord, we will ask Him to care for us. His supply will not leave us wanting but will fill us. His living water, His Spirit, draws us from the deep wells of grief and brings the comfort and grace only He can provide.

Hear our Lord saying: Get up and eat, for the journey is too much for you. I am your sustenance, your strength, your nourishment, and your peace that passes all understanding. I am your fulfillment in all things. Feed on My Word and take it into your soul.

Prayer

Oh my Father,

Thank you! You have granted peace and comfort to my broken heart. You are a great and mighty Savior. King of my heart! I am grateful for Your strength that carries me and for Your Word that fills my soul with the assurance of victory through You. I am so needy for You. I am desperate for You! Turn my discouragement from grief into faith in Your provisions. Guide me in the path You have chosen for me. Grant me a receptive heart and willing ear while I journey on.

God's Faithful Personal Promise

Write out Psalm 116:1–7

_____

_____

_____

_____

_____

Tammy's Story–The Mom

That's the Way It's Supposed to Be

Over five decades ago, God gave me life and breath. At three month of age, I was adopted into a Christian home. I received love, guidance, and a superior education. I attended college and graduate school. I got a good job. That job morphed into three more jobs to further my career. I met a special man and got married. I gave birth to Riley, a beautiful baby boy who was funny, smart, and talented. Up to this point, my life had been "the way it was supposed to be."

At the age of three, that sweet little boy began to have leg pains. Everyone said, "Those are just growing pains." He began to look a little pale. Then they said, "Maybe he has juvenile rheumatoid arthritis." He then caught an upper respiratory infection that just wouldn't go away. A special friend, who was a rheumatologist, had a suspicion that he had leukemia and sent us to a pediatric oncologist.

I remember the day in 1997 when they sat us down at a conference table in Charlotte, North Carolina, and told us that our son had neuroblastoma, a childhood cancer that at that time had about a 20 percent cure rate. The social worker said, "It isn't your fault."

When we asked the doctor what he would do, he said, "I hope I never have to make that decision." None of this advice was very helpful, so we went home to digest our new diagnosis, feeling helpless. This wasn't the way it was supposed to be!

God was already at work, and within a month, we were introduced to the team in Columbia, South Carolina, who would treat us for the next few years. Our primary doctor gave us two words of advice. First, put your back against the wall and come out fighting! Second, raise your child like he is going to collect Social Security. That is exactly what we did. This was the way it was supposed to be.

The next seven years were filled with treatments, a Children's Miracle Network adventure, a Make-A-Wish adventure, a skiing/snowboarding trip to Aspen with family, many new friends, and an education about a terminal disease that wasn't the way it was supposed to be. Riley was in remission for three years, and then the next round of bad news came. After a surgery and more rounds of chemo, we began a new regimen of treatments in New York City at Sloan Kettering Hospital, yielding a second period of remission and a "normal life." When the second relapse occurred, our options changed. We were now doing palliative care, giving him blood transfusions and treating the pain.

The day that hospice arrived at our house, Riley was ten years and twenty-four days old. God gave us a measure of grace, mercy, and peace that very day as he slipped away from us into the arms of God. This unexpected chapter of our life was over. We were now a family of three, with the challenge of starting over as our hearts healed.

Through it all, I have learned to do several things. First, I learned to accept help from friends and family. I learned to prioritize family and let the details take care of themselves. God also showed me what He had created me to do and gave me the strength to do it. Help came from unexpected places, and we had some of the best times of our lives while we were living at the Ronald McDonald House in Manhattan, New York.

My husband, my daughter, and I have grieved very differently. We have kept Riley's memory alive in our own ways. Ecclesiastes 7:3 says, "Sorrow is better than laughter, for sadness has a refining influence on us." Years later, I am just learning how to lament and wrestle with God over my brokenness so I can give Him control and resist the human urge to blame myself or others for my loss. This is all the result of God's grace and also "the way it is supposed to be."

Clara Ruth's Story–The Sister

Explaining death to a seven-year-old is the equivalent of explaining how a tomato is a fruit … and that's basically how my brain received the news that "Riley had died and gone home to be with Jesus."

While that was hard for me to understand at the time, I also had a limited scope of what "death" even meant. Was it a long vacation? And then people kept telling me I would see him once again. Wait, what? I understand the concept now, but I just couldn't wrap my head around it then. So many thoughts and emotions ran through my mind, but really, all I wanted to do was be with my family and process it together.

Seriously, the night after Riley died, family and friends gathered at our home, but after the whirlwind I had just been through, I refused to go inside until everyone was gone. In the midst of so many unfamiliar feelings, I wanted to be alone, and I wanted to feel normal … if that was even possible.

Fast-forward eleven years to my freshman year in college. I was eighteen and starting my first year at Baylor University. What should have been a year full of smiles, friendship, and new adventures was actually full of anxiety, tears, and uncertainty. After returning to a school closer to home for the spring semester, I told my mom that I just couldn't do it anymore. Just like the caring mother I've always known her to be, she referred me to a counselor, and I began to battle with years of hidden grief I didn't even realize existed.

I began to understand that because I was so young when Riley died, I never really had the opportunity to grieve, nor did I realize that I needed to. My mom was the driving force in our home, and she knew we had to get our lives back on track. It seemed like we never slowed down, but years later when I was a thousand miles away from home for the first time in my life, I had to put on the brakes and process what had happened years before.

The anxiety and uncertainty I was feeling then traced all the way back to the sadness and fear I felt when I lost my brother, my best friend. Once I was old enough to understand what these feelings meant, I was able to accept his death but also find hope in knowing he was pain-free and walking down the streets of gold.

For years, a particular passage in the Bible has always stood out to me. In 2 Timothy, Paul writes, "I have fought the good fight, I have kept the faith, and I have finished the race." Riley did that. He fought hard, so hard. He was faithful to the end, setting an incredible example for the rest of us, and he lived every day like it was his last. I couldn't even begin to tell you the number of people whose lives he impacted.

As for me, though, I'm almost certain Riley would want nothing more than for me to embody Paul's words. Genetically, we are both fighters. Spiritually, we are both faithful. Emotionally, we give it our all. While I might only be "twenty-two years young," as my grandmother says, I've got so much more life to live, and I intend to finish my race on a high note. I want to make him a proud brother, so I've got to keep going, and I find peace in knowing the Lord is with me every step of the way.[3]

Journal

Write your prayer of thankfulness to God for His provisions to you.

_____

_____

_____

_____

_____

_____

_____

_____

_____

_____

_____

_____

_____

_____

_____

_____

_____

_____

_____

Session 6

Faith in Shattered Hope

"What I feared has come upon me; what I dreaded has happened to me."
—Job 3:25

We don't yet see things clearly. We're squinting in a fog, peering
through a mist. But it won't be long before the weather clears
and the sun shines bright! We'll see it all then, see it all as clearly
as God sees us, knowing him directly just as he knows us!
—1 Corinthians 13:12 (MSG)

Look! There's the Shunammite! Run to meet her and ask her, "Are you
all right? Is your husband all right? Is your child all right?" "Did I ask
you for a son, my lord?" … "Didn't I tell you, 'Don't raise my hopes'?"
—2 Kings 4:25b and 28

T his journey in grief can be confusing. The tragic accident of my son's
passing goes over and over in my mind as I try to figure out exactly
what happened to cause him to fall out of the boat. No one knows

that answer except him and God. The whole occurrence of the accident, the loss, and life as it is now perplex me. Why and for what purpose? I long to see that massively large picture from beginning to end so I can understand why. This has been and is a hard journey and a mysterious one. I have seen God working through my loss in ways I had never seen God work before. I have witnessed Him orchestrate events that were obviously of His making. I am a recipient of many blessings in grace that have been poured out on me. It is strange that some blessings can only come through pain and suffering. When there is no understanding, God wants us to know He understands completely this journey we are on. We are limited in our discernment of how God works through such tragedies and loss.

How have you witnessed God working in your loss?

_____

_____

_____

God's ways are sometimes mysterious, even for those of us who have followed Him a long time. This story of a mother and son falls under that thought with me. For the story of the Shunammite woman, please read 2 Kings 4:8–37.

The Shunammite was a prominent and influential woman who, being hospitable, gave Elisha a place to stay when he was in town. She recognized him as a "holy man of God." Elisha, being pleased with his accommodations, wanted to do something for her, so he asked if he could speak on her family's behalf to the king or the commander of the army. Her reply tells us that she was content with her life just the way it was. She had everything she needed. She was not a greedy or selfish woman but one who was full of gratitude. However, Elisha's servant, Ghazi, suggested that since she was childless, she needed a son to carry on the family name and to leave an inheritance. So when Elisha told her she would have a son, her response implied there was a deep longing in her heart for a child. We are not told whether she had asked the Lord for a child, only that she was the recipient of God's grace.

As parents, we can surely relate to this elation of a much loved and wanted child. Our children become the focal point of our lives. Their needs come before ours. Everything we do seems to be centered on what is best for our child. They are a part of our flesh, our hearts, and our future. We watch them grow and learn and become their own person. They are our gracious gifts from God.

"I prayed for a child, You gave a child, then You take him back?" I can only imagine what was going on in the Shunammite's heart and mind as her son lay lifeless in her arms. Though we are not told, I believe she struggled with questions of her own. Why would God demonstrate so much grace and give her this child, then take him from her?

Notice the Shunammite didn't start preparing for a funeral. Instead, she laid her son on Elisha's bed and set out to find Elisha. Maybe she was thinking this man who God graciously worked through to give her a son might work to restore her son to life again. Ms. Shunammite knew the power of God came through Elisha. Without doubt, her relationship with the Lord had grown stronger because of Elisha's influence in her family's life. She had most likely heard the account of how God raised the widow's son during Elijah's time (1 Kings 17), and perhaps she recalled that miracle.

This woman showed great faith by her actions. Moreover, I find her actions to be with integrity. The first thing she does is go to her husband and informs him of a need to go to Elisha. This tells us she regards him as head of their family. Her husband, without even knowing why she must go, and in the kindness of his heart, does not prevent her from going and provides what she needs for the journey. In haste, she sets out to find Elisha. It was almost thirty miles from Shunem to Mt. Carmel where Elisha was staying. What was going through her mind? Did she cry all the way? Did she pray? Was she silent? Was she hopeful? Very likely all of these.

I would imagine Ms. Shunammite also felt fear as she hurried to Elisha. When she reached him, Elisha sent his servant, Ghazi, to her. "Are you all right? Is your husband all right? Is your child all right?"

"Everything is all right," she said. She dismissed Ghazi with this reply because it wasn't Ghazi she wanted to talk to. She wanted Elisha, that man of God. When we are in deep anguish of heart and soul, it is Jesus we should go to first. It is also good to have Christian friends or companions in grief to whom we can share our hearts.

We are not told in the scripture, but I like to imagine that when the Shunammite reached Elisha, she gave him all the details as she poured out her heart. He saw her bitter distress. Then came the questions from her anguished soul: "Did I ask you for a son, my Lord? Didn't I tell you, 'Don't raise my hopes'"? Why, God, why?

She would not leave until Elisha accompanied her. When they arrived, Elisha prayed first thing. This is an excellent example for all of us to always go to God first. This is His desire for us too. He is our heavenly Father wanting to help His child. Furthermore, we can only do what the power of God working through us can do. Then He receives all the glory.

Elisha was persistent in his prayer until the boy came back to life. Can you imagine the joy and relief of his mother when he was placed back into her arms! How grateful she was to God and the man of God! We have access to Almighty God through Jesus, our great high priest, and we too can pour out our hearts to Him. Whether it is thanksgiving and praise or heartache and sorrow, He is our loving heavenly Father and always worthy.

And so, God restored life to the Shunammite's son, and she was exceedingly grateful and acknowledged God through praising and thanking Him as she bowed down.

For a New Testament miracle, read Luke 8:41–50.

"Jairus, a ruler of the synagogue, came and fell at Jesus' feet, pleading with Him to come to his house because his only daughter, a girl of about twelve, was dying." Another version says Jairus was begging for Jesus to come. On Jesus's way there, the crowds were pushing against Him, wanting to see and hear. A miracle occurred amongst the mob of people, and a desperately ill woman was cured of her disease. This woman knew if she could just touch His cloak, His power could heal her. What great faith!

What about Jairus? *Hurry, Jesus, hurry!* Can you imagine the churning in his soul for Jesus to speed things along to help his dying daughter? The crowd was too much and slowing him down, and now they are stopping to see who touched Jesus! Jesus is never in a hurry. All through scripture, we never see Him rushing to do or to go, but He leisurely takes time for the needy. He has time in His hand.

Not realizing what had just happened, Jairus heard Jesus tell the woman, "Daughter, your faith has healed you. Go in peace." What an encouragement to hear! *Jesus was able to heal this woman; surely He could heal my daughter!* Suddenly the news came: "Don't bother the teacher anymore, Jairus. Your daughter is dead." What an emotional roller coaster he must have been on! One minute he is in haste, begging. Next, he certainly was frustrated at the delays and the crowd, followed by a miraculous healing and the most encouraging words he could hear. And now, tragic news!

I picture Jesus upon hearing this news, turning to look at Jairus, giving him His full attention with loving, compassionate eyes. Jesus said, "Don't be afraid; just believe, and she will be healed." *Don't be afraid.* Fear was my first emotion when the news came about my son. We are afraid of the unknown. We don't know what it is to die. Some of us may fear death or fear it for our loved ones. Jesus tells us, "Don't be afraid." He is the calm in our soul, the calm in our chaos.

Discuss a fear you might have experienced because of your loss.

_____

_____

_____

And so, Jesus restored life to Jairus's daughter, and everyone was astonished!

There is another mother and Son: Mary and Jesus. "Then Simeon blessed them and said to Mary, his mother: 'This child is destined to cause the falling and rising of many in Israel, and to be a sign that will be spoken against, so that the thoughts of many hearts will be revealed. And a sword will pierce your own soul too'" (Luke 2:34–35). Mary, as well as Jesus, would suffer deep anguish. She knew from the day of the angel's announcement that her Son was the Messiah. She pondered all that was said to her about Him in her heart. I can't imagine the agony she experienced of watching her Son be ridiculed, spit upon, hated, tortured, suffer, and die. It surely was a sword piercing her soul!

The good news is that God raised this Son from the grave! The significance of His rising is above all other resurrections and where our hope lies. Because Jesus lives, we too will live, forever (John 14:20). Without Christ's resurrection, our "faith is futile. But Christ has indeed been raised from the dead" (1 Corinthians 15:17, 20).

Jesus told His disciples that they would grieve over losing Him, but they would see Him again. And when they did, they would rejoice, and no one would take away their joy (John 16:22). No, this doesn't take away our grief, but it does point us to the one who can ease our pain and promise us lasting hope: the risen Christ!

In God's providence and mysterious ways, He chose to raise the son of the Shunammite and the daughter of Jairus. Jesus could have prevented my son's tragic accident had that been His will. Instead, He chose for me to trust my son's life to His care and know he is safe with other believers who are waiting for us to join them. Sometimes He chooses not to, and if that is your circumstance, "even if He does not" (Daniel 3:18 VOICE), will you remain faithful? He will always give us more of Himself, His compassion, His love, and sufficient grace to see us through. Like Simeon, we can look forward to the day we see Jesus and our believing loved ones.

In Acts 12, Herod had James, the brother of John, put to death. "When he (Herod) saw that it pleased the Jews, he proceeded to have Peter arrested as well" (verse 3 AMP). Later in the chapter, we find the believers meeting together and praying for Peter. While Peter was in prison in chains, an angel came and released him, and he was kept from suffering death at the hand of Herod. Now the question is, Why was James killed and Peter spared? I do not have the answer to that. I do know that God can be trusted with whatever circumstance we find ourselves in. He is faithful regardless of whether we understand or not.

Job struggled to understand the devastation that occurred in his life. Shortly after he loses everything, he so faithfully declares, "The LORD gave and the LORD has taken away; may the name of the LORD be praised" (Job 1:21). However, move forward two chapters, and we see his misery and complaints: "What I feared has come upon me; what I dreaded has happened to me. I have no peace, no quietness; I have no rest, but only turmoil" (Job 3:25–26). Zophar asked Job, "Do you think you can explain the mystery of God? Do you think you can diagram God Almighty?" (Job 11:7 MSG). We cannot know all of God. Deuteronomy 29:29 says, "The secret things belong to the LORD our God." Moreover, He is trustworthy, and Jesus has revealed what the Father is like. We cannot see His purposes from beginning to end, and neither could Job. "And we know (with great confidence) that God (who is deeply concerned about us) causes all things to work together (as a plan) for good for those who love God, to those who are called according to His plan *and* Purpose" (Romans 8:28 AMP).

Reading on in the book of Job, we see that he talked *to* God, not just about Him. He had a relationship with the living God and knew the one who could help his misery. God directed Job to His awesomeness and His holiness. No one compares to the Lord God Almighty. He doesn't have to give us an answer or a reason. He never explained Himself to Job. And Job declared, "Surely I spoke of things I did not understand, things too wonderful for me to know" (Job 42:3b). We have to know this too and believe and trust God in and through all things. Our afflictions are meant to drive us to our Bibles, to our knees, and nearer to God. Grief and sorrow are meant to strengthen our faith. From our loss, compassion grows stronger, love deeper, and our service valuable. Realizing the brevity of life, we should cherish our time, using it for the glory of God even in our sorrows.

God understands our complaints. I have definitely poured mine out to Him. I have read grief books that give the advice: *never ask God why.* Never question. So when our child or loved one dies, we are supposed to swallow our questions and never even think about them? Remember, God knows our thoughts. Our questions are wrong when our attitudes defy God and insist He answer to us for His ways. When I have asked questions of Him regarding my son's accident and death, I have received no reason or answers. I have, however, received more of God. I have more knowledge of His greatness and have acknowledged more of His character in my grief and loss. God is sovereign, and we are not. I can ask my questions to God, but I can also trust that He knows what He is doing in my life, and He knows what He is doing in yours.

Carol's story shares how she believes God can use her loss for His good even when she does not understand. Let her story at the end of this session give you hope.

Our hearts have been pierced from losing our precious loved ones. Although God's ways are sometimes mysterious, if we "dwell in the secret place of the Most High" (Psalm 91:1 NKJV), we will find our stability in knowing God never changes, nor does His love for us. Trust God with your aching soul and rest with the calm assurance that His healing can come through many ways, and death is one of them. Never again will the believers who were mentally or physically ill or died in tragic accidents experience sickness, death, or tragedies in any form. They have been eternally healed! They have been raised from death to new life! I have at times even been relieved that I do not have to worry about my son anymore. He is safe! That is worth our praise and thanksgiving to our God today and every day until we join them.

God's Faithful Personal Promise

Write out 1 Peter 1:3–9

_____

_____

_____

Even through sorrow, God is worthy of our praise. He has graced us with a living hope because of Christ's resurrection. Our suffering tests our faith and grows us to stand firm. One day we will see that massive picture. We will understand all that we do not now understand. We will see it all unfold and how God gloriously worked everything for His good purposes (Romans 8:28). Our inheritance is kept safe for us, and our faith will have sight upon arrival there. When we finally do arrive in heaven and our trials are over, praise, glory, and honor will go on forever! We will have made it safely home.

Journal Quote:

> When I lay these questions before God I get no answer. But a rather special sort of "No answer." It is not the locked door. It is more like a silent, certainly not uncompassionate, gaze. As though He shook His head not in refusal but waiving the question. Like, "Peace, child; you don't understand."[1] (C. S. Lewis, *A Grief Observed*)

Carol's Story

My journey began July 25, 1991. My only child, a son, Chris, was killed in an auto accident at the age of twenty-four.

Some would say twenty-five years is a long time, but some days it seems like yesterday.

Every day, I miss him and grieve for him, and I still wonder, *Why?* But I know God makes no mistakes, so I trust Him in *all* things. One thing I am sure of is God's grace is sufficient for me (2 Corinthians 12:9), so until He takes me home to be reunited with Chris, it will continue to be!

It has taken many years and an ocean of tears, but at this place in my journey, I thank God for giving me the honor and privilege of being Chris's mom!

"All things work together for good to them that love God, to them who are the called according to his purpose" (Romans 8:28 KJV). I don't understand this, but I have to believe it!

Please remember this: God's compassions never fail, and they are "new every morning: Great is thy faithfulness" (Lamentations 3:22–23 KJV).[2]

Journal

Session 7

Your Book Is Being Written

You have decided the length of our lives. You know how many
months we will live, and we are not given a minute longer.
—Job 14:5 (NLT)

All the days ordained for me were written in your
book before one of them came to be.
—Psalm 139:16b

This God is our God forever and ever. He will
lead us from now to the end of time!
—Psalm 48:14 (ERV)

H ere we are at this place in our lives. This is not how we dreamed
our life would turn out. We would not have chosen this path of
grief and loss. The intense love we have for those we have lost
will always be with us. Although a part of us has died, we continue to live
on. We cannot escape life's difficulties or heartaches. Jesus said, "In the

world you have tribulation and distress and suffering" (John 16:33 AMP). However, the very next comment Jesus makes is what this study is all about: To keep us from giving up. To strengthen us to forge ahead, trusting in the one who is able to carry us all the way. Jesus said, "But be courageous (be confident, be undaunted, be filled with joy); I have overcome the world." Praise God for this promise! Someone has said, "God will examine your life not for medals, diplomas, or degrees but for battle scars."

The verses at the beginning of this session make clear that our days are in the hands of God and are numbered. We don't know when our time on earth will be up and we will experience our last day. However, God does know, and that should be comforting to us. I take comfort believing that God knew the day of my son's passing before he was even born, and his purpose in life was achieved.

One day, the memories will be more than the grief. For a while, our grief is all we know. We can't see past it. We are disoriented. Gradually, we start moving out of the muddle. I believe we never fully recover from grief this side of heaven. Grief takes time; let it work by asking its questions, enduring the agony, demanding its way. We learn to live with it, in it, and because of it. Grief becomes part of who we now are.

I have always had a big laugh and smile with my whole face. After my son passed away, there was no heart for laughter. I'm not sure how much time had passed, but I remember the first time I laughed after my son's passing. I have this funny little Jack Russell dog with big ears that stand straight up. She has obvious facial expressions. When she looks at me and I speak, her ears lay back, and she smiles with her eyes. I don't even remember what she did on this day, but it was so funny that I laughed out loud. I had not laughed in so long that the unexpected sound of my laughter surprised me. My first thought was, *Gary hears me laughing.* Instead of feeling guilty or disrespectful, I felt it was what he would want to hear, and it was all right. Some of us may think that to laugh or rejoin life is being disrespectful to the ones we have lost. Our loved ones would want us to be happy, to live and laugh. They know we will always love and remember them.

We cannot let our grief rob us of our joy. We have to give our hearts and minds rest from the heartache to see life again. I'm writing this in late spring. The flowers are blooming, the birds are singing, and the trees have thankfully turned green again. There is new life everywhere. There are things we can do to help ourselves: Take a walk. Plant some flowers. Sew a garment. Work on a craft. Read a good, uplifting book. Have lunch with a friend. Offer to help someone else going through a hard time. I have found strength by helping others, even in small ways. Two weeks after my son's accident, a friend's mother passed away. I felt the need to take them food. Ed and I had been the recipients of many meals in those two weeks. I wanted to show someone else the same comfort I had been given by offering a meal. Yes, I was consumed in my grief, but I found the drive to help someone else.

Discouragement is a weapon used by the enemy to keep us from going forward. Of course, we will have times when we feel this way, but know we cannot stay there. Moreover, discouragement is a thief that robs us of joy and peace. We must recognize this when it comes barreling into our lives and by God's grace work through discouragement.

> Do not yield to discouragement no matter how severely stressed or surrounded by problems you may be. A discouraged soul is in a helpless state, being neither able to "stand against the devil's schemes" (Ephesians 6:11) himself nor able to prevail in prayer for others. Flee every symptom of the deadly foe of discouragement, as you would run from a snake. Never be slow to turn your back on it, unless you desire to eat the dust of bitter defeat.[1]
> (*Streams in the Desert*)

The first year of my loss, I took up jewelry making. I had been learning the trade before my son's accident, but that year before Christmas, I became engrossed in making gifts of jewelry. This act kept me busy and was a relief for a while from the misery. I guess you could say it gave me an escape from my thoughts and also gave me joy when I presented each carefully made gift. Allowing ourselves to enjoy the simple things in life brings us a more hopeful outlook.

For years, I walked for exercise and as fast as I could to get my heart rate up and burn more calories. After my son's death, there was no motivation or incentive to walk or exercise in any form. I vividly remember one day walking up our back yard and suddenly realizing that my shoulders were slumped, and my pace was almost to a crawl. The heaviness I felt from the grief was weighing my body and soul down. For the next four years, I was like this. My body ached even to the touch. My chest ached from grief, and it seemed like life had been sucked out of me. Slowly, and after a few more years, I straightened my shoulders and took a new interest in walking. I don't walk as fast as I used to. It is more of a thoughtful enjoyment walk that revives my mind and soul. It feels good to just walk!

Share how you have found, or you would like to find, ways to give your grief a rest.

_____

_____

_____

_____

Our deepest joy comes from God. It comes from a personal relationship with Jesus. Happiness is based on circumstances. Happiness disappears when life becomes sorrowful. Joy is continual no matter what our lot in life. James 1:2–4 (VOICE) says that we will find joy in our hardships. I used to cringe when I read these verses, but the more I read them and soaked in the words, I began to know from experience what James is saying. "Don't run from tests and hardships, brothers and sisters. As difficult as they are, you will ultimately find joy in them; if you embrace them, your faith will blossom under pressure and teach you true patience as you endure. And true patience brought on by endurance will equip you to complete the long journey and cross the finish line— mature, complete, and wanting nothing." Find joy in our hardships? Embrace them? Find patience? Yes, even when we don't feel like it. It is the supernatural work of God. By accepting our sorrow, and this takes time, we can allow God to work in and through our grief for His great purposes. It is a surrender of our lives to Christ. *Not my will, Lord, but Yours be done for Your glory and praise.* By staying true to God, we find strength to keep going. We find joy from the confident assurance we have in salvation and hope in Jesus. This is true joy. Therefore, our faith grows because of our afflictions, and God equips us with everything we need to finish our journey.

Do you believe that God has everything you need for this journey? Why or why not?

_____

_____

_____

Read and think on these verses and this statement: the condition to our receiving is believing.

- o   Matthew 21:22
- o   Romans 4:20–21
- o   Philippians 4:19
- o   Ephesians 3:20

Faithfully stay in the Word of God. Your Bible is real. The stories are about real people and their real lives. God is living and real. The words are inspired by God and help us in every way (2 Timothy 3:16–17). We can trust them. We can live by them. "Forever, O LORD, Your word is settled in heaven (standing firm and unchangeable). Your faithfulness continues from generation to generation" (Psalm 119:89 AMP).

Faithfully stay in prayer. God said in 1 Samuel 13:14 and Acts 13:22 that David was a man after God's own heart. Reading through the Psalms David wrote, we see his relationship with the living God. Although his life had trouble, heartache, and grief, David stayed in communication with God and learned to sing praises through it all. Psalm 40 is a great example of this.

Read Psalm 40.

David humbled himself. He waited patiently for God to give him relief from the pit of despair. He acknowledged that God hears him. God lifts David out of his misery and gives security. He is given a new song, a hymn of praise to our God. David desires to do God's will.

Aren't you encouraged that David wrote from his heart so that thousands of years later we could relate and be comforted? Record other hopeful phrases you see in Psalm 40.

_____

_____

_____

"After you have suffered a little while, our God, who is full of kindness through Christ, will give you his eternal glory. He personally will come and pick you up, and set you firmly in place, and make you stronger than ever" (1 Peter 5:10 TLB). "March on, my soul; be strong!" (Judges 5:21b).

I want to be a woman after God's own heart. Our pastor said, "The making of a man or woman of God is in the prayer closet." In our sorrow, and perhaps even more so because of it, remain faithful in prayer.

So, we cannot let grief rob us of our joy. What is more, we cannot let grief rob us of our peace. Peace is a gift from God. Inner peace, the kind from God, exceeds all understanding and guards our hearts and our minds in Christ Jesus (Philippians 4:7). Before Jesus went to heaven, He promised the believers many things. He promised He would send the Holy Spirit to live in us. Jesus referred to Him as a comforter and a counselor to be with us forever. He also said the Holy Spirit is truth.

Jesus promised that He was preparing us a place to live in heaven and that one day He is coming back to take us there. And Jesus promised us peace. His peace. "I do not give to you as the world gives. Do not let your hearts be troubled and do not be afraid" (John 14:2–3 and 27).

God's peace is essential. "You will keep in perfect and constant peace the one whose mind is steadfast (that is, committed and focused on You—in both inclination and character), because he trusts and takes refuge in You (with hope and confident expectation)" (Isaiah 26:3 AMP). Another great and remarkable promise of God that also has conditions! As believers, this should be our aim. During hard and raw grief, this takes a deliberate act of will. This is the time to take refuge in God. Let Him hold you in His arms and tenderly comfort you with His peace. He will restore hope and confident expectation to your weary soul. Peace is a gift from God.

Reflect on Romans 15:13: "May the God of hope fill you with all joy and peace as you trust in him, so that you may overflow with hope by the power of the Holy Spirit."

We have learned that joy and peace that are from God stand firm in the face of grief and loss. They are unwavering in all of life's tough circumstances. Moreover, when joy and peace dwell in our hearts, we are able to give praise to God. When Job learned that he had lost his children, his servants, and his livestock, the first thing he did was fall to the ground in worship and blessed the name of the Lord (Job 1:20–21). And when David learned his son with Bathsheba had died, he went to the house of the Lord and worshipped. Regardless of our circumstances, God is always worthy of our praise. Praise honors Him.

"When they had sung a hymn, they went out to the Mount of Olives" (Matthew 26:30).

We can read verses of scripture many times over, and one day a certain verse will jump off the page with a deeper sense of the meaning than we've ever had before. This verse from Matthew recently affected me differently. Directly after the disciples and Jesus met in the upper room, they sang a hymn. Jesus sang a hymn knowing all that was about to take place: he would be arrested, ridiculed, put on trial, spit upon, beaten, tortured, rejected by His friends, crucified, have the sins of the world laid on His shoulders, and be separated from His Father and death. Jesus sang a hymn. How utterly amazing!

In Acts 16:22–25, Paul and Silas had been arrested and put in prison but not before they were stripped and beaten, severely flogged, and put in the inner cell, with their feet fastened in stocks. Lying in a cold, damp, filthy prison cell, they "were praying and singing hymns to God, and the other prisoners were listening to them" (verse 25). How could they have possibly done this? By holding on to their joy. Their joy was not in their circumstances but in God, the one who could comfort and sustain them. This is the kind of joy that keeps us singing and praying even in the midst of our sorrows. Our response to our grief is being watched by a lost world. Will we cling to our God and praise Him even in our pain or will we fall into the realms of total despair? Because of Paul and Silas's faithfulness, the jailer and his whole family became believers! Stay faithful! Don't give up!

In our grief, there are times when we don't feel like singing praises. In the darkness, Jesus will be our light that draws us to Him. Psalm 42 is a beautiful illustration of being in a despairing place in our souls yet knowing God is pulling us back to praising Him.

Read Psalm 42 and record a verse or verses that minister to your heart.

_____

_____

_____

For me, it is verse 11: "Why are you downcast, O my soul? Why so disturbed within me? Put your hope in God, for I will yet praise him, my Savior and my God."

Praise will help us get through. There is always something to praise God for. His blessings are immeasurable. Where would we be without His grace, love, and mercy?

Yes, He is worthy of praise, in good times and in hard times.

List some of the blessings you have received while in your grief that enables you to give God praise.

_____

_____

_____

If our eyes are open and our hearts receptive, this space is not adequate to write how blessed we are.

The end session story is from my sweet friend Janice. Throughout her journey in loss, she knew and trusted in the one who would provide all she needed. Her story is a beautiful illustration of a faithful and loving God working in her life.

"Now He came near the path down the Mount of Olives, and the whole crowd of the disciples began to praise God joyfully with a loud voice for all the miracle they had seen: The King who comes in the name of the Lord is the blessed One. Peace in heaven and glory in the highest heaven! Some of the Pharisees from the crowd told Him, 'Teacher, rebuke Your disciples.' He answered, 'I tell you, if they were to keep silent, the stones would cry out!'" (Luke 19:37–40 Holman). Wow! God *will be* praised! And I want to be part of His creation that is offering up praise for all He is and has done for me.

> Then I looked and heard the voice of many angels, numbering thousands upon thousands, and ten thousand times ten thousand. They encircled the throne and the living creatures and the elders. In a loud voice they sang: "Worthy is the Lamb, who was slain, to receive power and wealth and wisdom and strength and honor and glory and praise!" Then I heard every creature in heaven and on earth and under the earth and on the sea, and all that is in them, singing: "To him who sits on the throne and to the Lamb be praise and honor and glory and power, for ever and ever!" (Revelation 5:12–13)

Hold on to your joy, your peace, and your praise. Be comforted knowing the relationships with our believing loved ones who have gone before us have not ended but are only postponed. It is a temporary separation. We will embrace them again, never to be separated, and we will know complete joy. We will have complete peace. Paul said in 1 Thessalonians 4:13 (NLT), "We want you to know what will happen to the believers who have died so you will not grieve like people who have no hope." Notice he didn't say not to grieve, because we are going to grieve for our loved ones. But he is saying to grieve with hope. We, as Christians, have life everlasting, and our lives and grief should reflect this hope. Furthermore, verses 14–18 tell us that all who trust Christ will one day be relieved of life's sorrows, and we are to encourage each other with these truths.

"Where, O death, is your victory? Where, O death, is your sting?" (1 Corinthians 15:55).

"He will swallow up death forever" (Isaiah 25:8). This is worth praising God for!

Here we are at the end of our study. Looking back over these weeks, we have covered so much about grief and loss, sorrow and pain, and how to move on while still living this out. We've also looked at many attributes of God and the help He offers us. Let's look at some of them.

God is

- our ever-present God who never leaves us or forsakes us,
- our Shepherd who carefully watches over us and nurtures our souls,
- our guardian as Father, husband, and friend,
- good,
- our Redeemer,
- holy,
- faithful,
- merciful,
- companion in sorrow,
- our strength,
- our Deliverer,
- our Provider,
- a compassionate God,
- the bread of life and living water,
- the God of power and resurrection,
- our joy,
- our peace
- our comfort.

And He is so much more! Isn't He worthy of our praise and worship?

At the beginning of this session, one of our verses was Psalm 48:14: "This God is our God forever and ever. He will lead us from now to the end of time." I pray that as you stay in His Word and in prayer, keeping your eyes fixed on Him, that you will see Him guiding you through life. "Thus far has the Lord helped us" (1 Samuel 7:12b). Look back on your journey and see how the Lord has helped you. Look at today and see how He is covering you with His grace. Look forward because we are still on this journey. We may have many more miles to go. We may have more to endure down the road—more sorrows, more losses. Take heart! We have our all-sufficient God to walk this road with us. Furthermore, we have so much to look forward to! One day, our God "will wipe every tear from (our) eyes. There will be no more death or mourning or crying or pain, for the old order of things has passed away" (Revelation 21:4). So take hold of our Savior! Be brave! Be courageous! Be strong! "Thus far has the Lord helped us," and He will until the end of time!

God's Faithful Personal Promise

Write out Psalm 119:49–50

_____

_____

_____

Write out 2 Chronicles 16:9

_____

Fix your heart on Jesus. Trust in Him.

Journal Quote:

The Lord who "thus far" has helped you will help you all your journey through.

Janice's Story

June 30, 1972, was the happiest day of my life. My husband, Ted, and I became parents to a beautiful baby girl we named Vanessa. She was my greatest joy, and I was blessed to be her mother for twenty-four years.

After graduating college, she had many plans for her future, including hiking the Appalachian Trail. She was an outdoor enthusiast, which is one thing we did not have in common. She loved all of God's creation and enjoyed exploring and experiencing His wonders as often as she could. Ted and I know we cannot live her dream, but we often go places we know she visited and hiked.

December 21, 1996, was the day that changed my life forever. Ted and I received the call that every parent fears. Our Vanessa had died in a house fire. Nothing can prepare you for the intense pain you experience after losing a child. It is God's grace that makes grief bearable.

Since losing Vanessa, our focus has been on fire safety. We did not want another family to go through what we did if it could be prevented. Five years after her death, Ted was reading the job ads in our paper and saw that our city was hiring a fire inspector and public educator. He had not been looking for a job, but he had been working with the fire department on a smoke detector program. The house in which Vanessa died did not have working smoke detectors. He applied for the job, and although he had no experience in the fire service, he was hired. This new job gave new meaning to our lives. We were able to directly affect others who might not have smoke detectors in their homes and also enforce codes requiring smoke detectors in public and private housing. That also included college dorms and schools. God knew that it would take time to heal, in order to be effective at a job that was a constant reminder of our daughter's death. God's timing was perfect. We have found a sense of purpose because of this opportunity. "Trust in the Lord with all thine heart; and lean not unto thine own understanding. In all Thy ways acknowledge Him, and He shall direct Thy paths" (Proverbs 3:5–6 KJV).

I am a Christian, and I knew that God would provide whatever and whomever I needed to get through this terrible tragedy. "It is of the Lord's mercies that we are not consumed, because His compassions fail not. They are new every morning: great is Thy faithfulness" (Lamentations 3:22–23 KJV).

God knew my needs and met them through the love of family, friends, church family, and even strangers. He also provided those who I refer to as "friends for a season." They met whatever need I had during the different stages of my grief. I received cards of both sympathy and encouragement every week for months, and some continued for years. Just knowing others were lifting me up in prayer gave me the strength to go on and not give up.

"Blessed are they that mourn: for they shall be comforted" (Matthew 5:4 KJV).

In the seasons that break us, the hand of God is shaping us.

When Ted and I chose Vanessa's name, we did not know what a source of comfort it would bring twenty-four years later. It was only after her death that we learned her name means "butterfly." The butterfly symbolizes renewed life and hope. Like the butterfly, I believe I emerged from my cocoon of grief, transformed into a better person. God is faithful to send me signs of hope and assurance that Vanessa is still among us even though she is in heaven. On June 29, 2002, the day before Vanessa's thirtieth birthday, Ted and I were taking trash to his office building and were not able to get close to the dumpster. As we walked through the grass, a small piece of paper caught my eye. The paper was ripped and tattered, but on it was a penciled drawing of a butterfly and a flower. Not just any flower but her favorite flower, a tulip. Look for the signs. God is so good.

I read this quote during the early stages of my grief and I share it often: "God never wastes a hurt! Your greatest ministry will most likely come out of your greatest hurt." My prayer is that my story will help others find hope in the midst of their grief.[2]

Journal

Leader Guide

Because grief can be overwhelming, exhausting, and consuming, this study is written with that in mind and heart. Too much to take in can be as wearisome as having nothing to lean on. There is only one session to complete during each week, allowing participants time to gather their thoughts and focus on the prayerfully thought-out scriptures, questions, and God's faithful promises. Time is needed for contemplation and absorption.

If you are facilitating a group, plan a two-hour session each week for a total of seven weeks. Be creative and caring. Providing coffee and refreshments is a good way to break the ice with participants, making them feel welcome. Have an introduction time. Start each session in prayer. Pray during the week for your group that the Lord will guide their thoughts to Him. The gospel message is given in session 3. Pray for those who may be lost in your group.

Other suggestions would be to share an opening song or poem, one that pertains to that week's study. Encourage each member and generate discussions from the session questions and God's promises taught that week (examples below).

Allow participants ample time to talk out their journey and understand that some may never say a word, and that's okay, as we all deal with grief differently. At the same time, realize you are on a time schedule and be responsible with discussions. We can grow more hopeful from our conversations with each other. At the end of each session, highlight the heartening and inspiring ways they learned to persevere for the days ahead. Remember, grief is life changing, and some may be trying to catch their breath for the next moment. Knowing that they are not alone and that God is continually with them is paramount.

There are spaces for comments and thoughts throughout the study. Encourage the participants to take advantage of these spaces and to write them out. Placed at the end of each session are "God's Faithful Personal Promises" and a journal section. The promises have been prayerfully thought through to comfort their hearts and take hold of the promises: clinging to the words, hiding them in their hearts. The journal is provided for their daily thoughts, prayers, and feelings. Writing out their personal journey is an authentic way of seeing God moving in their lives. Reflecting back over time will help them see progression in their grief and God's beautiful, amazing grace covering them. Only when I became transparent and honest with God and wrote out the deep hurt that was heaped up inside me did I discover that it was necessary for me to be vulnerable in order for others to be able to relate to their own hurt and grief. When we do this pouring out, whether in conversation or on paper, we help each other, and we together share in God's grace. Again, the journal is provided but not required.

Listen to what the group contributes and do not forget to add what the Lord may be teaching you throughout the Bible study. Sharing prayer needs and praying for one another during the week are good ways to connect. Their relationship with Jesus is of utmost importance.

Discussion

Session 1

What are your hopes in doing this study?

Discuss this statement: You are not alone because God will "never leave you or forsake you"; however, sometimes your loneliness can be rooted in the fact that you are not in fellowship with Jesus.

Does the journal quote encourage you while being together in this group?

Session 2

This week, you were asked to read from Psalm 139 and Matthew 10:29–31. How does God's omnipresence and omniscience bring peace to your circumstances?

Psalm 139:16 states that our days are ordained, appointed for each of us. Discuss how this verse can bring comfort to those whose lives seemed to be cut short.

Session 3

What does it mean to give your sorrow to God, trusting Him when all seems dark?

Jesus said in John 14:1, "Do not let your heart be troubled." Discuss this command.

Session 4

From my experience concerning the cow and her calf, what odd—or maybe not odd at all—circumstances have come into your life that caused you grief, due to being separated from your loved one?

Hard question: How do you minister to someone whose loved one was not a believer and who is experiencing separation anxiety? What scriptures can be found to bring comfort? I heard someone say once that we do not know for sure who is in hell because at their last breath, they may have cried out to Jesus for salvation, like the thief on the cross. However, we are sure of many who are in heaven.

Session 5

How hard is it to rely on God when you feel numb?

Have you experienced harsh reactions to your grief journey from family members or friends who grieve differently than you?

What does "one day at a time" or "one moment at a time" mean to you at this point in your journey?

Session 6

Discussion comment: If you are a believer, God is *always* working on your behalf. He never works against you. It is *always* for your good.

The book of Job is very relatable for those in deep grief. How does reading his journey help you to carry on?

Session 7

How can we allow sorrow and loss to inspire us to help others and drive us for ministry?

What are some ways this study may have changed the way you see your circumstances?

Looking back, in hindsight, how have you seen God working in your life?

Notes

Session 1: You Are Not Alone

1. Janet Lindsey, *Peering through a Mist*.
2. Janet Lindsey, *Therefore, Hope*.
3. Martha Whitmore Hickman, *I Will Not Leave You Desolate* (Abingdon Press, 1994).
4. Used by permission from Becky Sewell.

Session 2: God Is Good, So Why Has This Happened?

1. Janet Lindsey, *Peering through a Mist*.
2. Janet Lindsey, *Therefore, Hope*.
3. Billy Graham, *Hope for Each Day* (Thomas Nelson, 2002).
4. Oswald Chambers, *My Utmost for His Highest*, ed. James Reimann (Oswald Chambers Publications Assn., Ltd., 1992. Used by permission of Discovery House, Grand Rapid, MI 49501. All rights reserved.
5. Used by permission from Ed Russell.

Session 3: Be Not Paralyzed

1. Janet Lindsey, *Therefore, Hope*.

2. Susan Duke, *Grieving Forward* (2006). Used by permission of Warner Faith Hachette Book Group USA. All rights reserved.

3. Used by permission from Rosemary Anna.

4. Used by permission from Gary Christian.

Session 4: Lost and Separated

1. J. C. Ryle, bishop of Liverpool.

2. Used by permission from Brandi Trent.

Session 5: The Journey Is Too Much for You

1. Janet Lindsey, *Therefore, Hope.*

2. Used by permission from Tammy West.

3. Used by permission from Clara Ruth West.

Session 6: Faith in Shattered Hope

1. C. S. Lewis, *A Grief Observed* (C. S. Lewis Pte. Ltd., 1961). Extract reprinted by permission.

2. Used by permission from Carol Whitehead.

Session 7: Your Book Is Being Written

1. L. B. Cowman, *Streams in the Desert* (Zondervan, 1997). Used by permission of Zondervan, www.zondervan.com.

2. Used by permission from Janice Williams.

About the Author

J anet Lindsey is a passionate author who is intent on helping others in their grief process. Janet knows from experience that reading the pages of scripture and pouring our hearts out to God are how comfort and strength will come. She wants others to know that they can not only survive in their loss but also use it to bring others to a saving knowledge of Jesus Christ. Janet has learned that there are hurting people everywhere who need to be encouraged to keep the faith and grow through the trials they are enduring. She offers hope in what can sometimes seem like hopeless circumstances. Her writing is a message to all those who seek solace and purpose through afflictions.

Janet has authored two books on grief and God's amazing grace. In *Peering through a Mist,* Janet shares her struggles to understand the questions left unanswered. Her transparency has helped others to know they are not alone in their anguish. While writing *Therefore, Hope,* the author recognized her progression in grief compared to her first book. Janet offers hope in Jesus through heartache and pain. Moreover, she has experienced firsthand His graciousness with her.

Janet utilizes blogging to demonstrate God's perpetual working through grief and loss. Opportunities occur continuously, which spur the next blog. You may find her blog at janetlindsey.blogspot.com.

Janet and her husband, Ed, of thirty-three years, host a mega fishing tournament every summer in memory of their son who passed away from a fishing accident. With upwards of two hundred boats, they have opportunities to minister to others in grief and give back to worthy organizations, most of which are involved with search and rescue. For more information on the tournament, go to www.garylindsey.net.

Printed in the United States
By Bookmasters